Welles-Turner Memorial Library
2407 Main Street
Glastonbury, Connecticut 06033

In memory of

William "Sam" Kowalsky

and

Dorothy S. Kowalsky

Haynes

Aquarium
Manual

First published in October 2009

British Library Cataloguing in Publication Data
A catalogue record for this book is available from the British Library

ISBN 978 1 84425 640 2

Library of Congress control no. 2009927969

Published by Haynes Publishing,
Sparkford, Yeovil, Somerset BA22 7JJ, UK
Tel: 01963 442030 Fax: 01963 440001
Int. tel: +44 1963 442030 Int. fax: +44 1963 440001
E-mail: sales@haynes.co.uk
Website: www.haynes.co.uk

Haynes North America Inc.
861 Lawrence Drive, Newbury Park,
California 91320, USA

Printed and bound in the UK

Credits

Author:	**Jeremy Gay**
Project Manager:	**Louise McIntyre**
Copy editor:	**Ian Heath**
Page design:	**James Robertson**
Index:	**Peter Nicholson**
Photography:	
Neil Hepworth	
George Farmer	
Photomax	
Practical Fishkeeping	
Aquajardin (Samuel Baker)	
Aquapress	
Rolf. C. Hagen (UK) Ltd.	
Illustrations:	**Matthew Marke**

Haynes

Aquarium
Manual

The complete step-by-step guide to keeping fish

Jeremy Gay

USEFUL TIPS ON SETTING UP, FILTRATION, FISH HEALTH, EQUIPMENT, MAINTENANCE

CONTENTS

Welcome to the world of fishkeeping!

By picking up this book you have already shown an interest in what can be a fascinating and rewarding hobby. Maybe you've bought an aquarium and wish to find out more about the fish that are living inside it, or maybe you want to keep a pet and are exploring your options? Either way, as you flick through the pages you'll get an inkling of what this hobby entails, and how diverse and rich the natural world is below the waterline.

Fishkeeping can be as easy or as complex as you want it to be, and suits people of all ages, all budgets and all abilities. No other hobby or pastime – or pet, for that matter – combines art, science, geography and relaxation like fishkeeping does, and with thousands of fish species to choose from there will always be that perfect fish to suit your personal taste and needs.

Perfect pets

Fish don't need to be cuddled or taken for walks, and if you go away on holiday they wont miss you. All they require from you is a little care and attention, to be kept well fed, and to have their water kept free of pollution. If you have some spare time, a little money and the willingness to learn, you can be fishkeeping within weeks of making the decision to own an aquarium and keep fish.

Many people were first introduced to fish as children, with a humble goldfish in a bowl. Many may be reminded of such a childhood experience when they see fish, or may just be wowed by the colours and diversity of fish when they see them in their thousands in an aquarium shop. But whether it's a goldfish, some Neon tetras, or even a Piranha that takes

your fancy, by deciding to keep them you have embarked on what will prove a truly fulfilling hobby.

A world of choice

Better understanding of the needs of fish combined with better technology now enable us to keep almost any fish in aquariums, from the very small to the very large, and naturally inhabiting a myriad of different conditions. Most aquarium shops stock coldwater fish, tropical freshwater fish, and tropical marine fish that inhabit coral reefs in tropical oceans.

The three types vary in cost, requirements and variety, and if you become truly hooked on fishkeeping, as many thousands of people have all around the world, one fish tank may soon turn into several, and you may end up keeping coldwater, tropical *and* marine!

Beyond the constraints of space there is no limit to the number of fish or aquariums that you can keep, and by treating your fish well they will reward you with many years of relaxing viewing. They may even breed. If procreation is your thing, how about the live-bearing guppy, a small, colourful, tropical fish that is easy to keep and gives birth to live young? Breeding fish can mean a special event for most, and it is a great educational tool too.

Green-fingered fishkeepers can grow plants in their aquariums too, and arrange them in stunning underwater gardens that provide their fish with optimum conditions and provide a view that will grace any living space.

For the ultimate challenge, and an ultimate demonstration of Nature's beauty, marine fish are hard to beat, and when provided with perfect conditions you can keep not only the fish but also the corals, shrimps, crabs and starfish that live alongside them on the reef. Nothing can beat a well-decorated marine tank, brimming with life from top to bottom.

Whatever type of aquarium you choose, above all you should enjoy it. Make time not just to maintain and look after your fish but also to sit back and enjoy the fruits of your labour. Fishkeeping is a constant commitment, but one that will go on to reward you time and time again. Experienced fishkeepers can go on to become experts in a very short time, and will then be able to share their knowledge and experience with others.

The *Haynes Aquarium Manual* is packed full of pictures and information that will help to get you started, and provides you with everything you need to know about aquarium fish and how to keep them.

THE
AQUARIUM

Selection

With so much choice, where do you start? By visiting your local aquatic shop you'll no doubt get an idea of which fish you want to keep. It will usually be something very colourful, unusually shaped, or full of character and almost gesturing at you, saying 'Buy me, buy me'!

But not all fish can live happily together in an aquarium. Some grow larger than others and may scare them, some fish eat other fish, and marine fish must be housed in a different aquarium altogether, filled with synthetic seawater.

Then there's the question of your means, budget and abilities. A goldfish is cheap to buy, fairly easy to keep and won't take up too much of your time maintaining it. A Clownfish is more expensive to buy, its aquarium set-up is more technical and expensive, and its maintenance is more complicated. Or you could settle for tropical community fish, which are somewhere in between.

Tropical, coldwater or marine?

This will be the first major decision to make when starting out with fish, as the three different types cannot be kept together. As mentioned above, these three types have different start-up costs and levels of maintenance; but they'll also need different equipment, and possibly even different aquariums.

Coldwater fish

Coldwater fish usually means a goldfish, or a few other species that don't need to be kept in heated aquariums. They're easy to keep and are long-lived, though as goldfish can grow to a foot or more they need a spacious aquarium. Goldfish come in a number of varieties, though in terms of the number of species available there are few.

WHAT YOU NEED TO KNOW ABOUT COLDWATER FISH
Because they grow large and eat a lot goldfish produce a lot of waste, meaning that you'll need adequate filtration to deal with this. They're generally very docile and don't fight with each other, though the short-bodied fancy goldfish varieties may be attacked by other fish. Although often kept in bowls, a medium to large aquarium is the only proper way to keep them.

Tropical fish

Tropical fish come in a huge range of colours, shapes and varieties, and thousands of species are available. These vary in size, cost and ease of keeping, and constitute the most popular type of fishkeeping due to their huge variety. Even if you only have a tiny aquarium there's a tropical fish species to suit, and many community species are no more difficult to keep than a goldfish.

Tropical fishkeeping can be subdivided into many different areas, like planted aquariums, cichlid keeping and Discus keeping. At the top end of the scale, some tropical fish can rival marine fish for colour, cost and the skill required to keep them.

WHAT YOU NEED TO KNOW ABOUT TROPICAL FISH

Unless you live in a hot country, tropical fish need artificially heated aquariums, so the cost of buying a heater and running one must be included in your budget. With so many species to choose from, not all will mix, so do your homework on species compatibility.

Marine fish

Marine fish come in the brightest colours and strangest patterns of all. Because of the exacting conditions of tropical oceans they live within very narrow tolerances, so are regarded as the most difficult to keep of the three aquarium types. They also take up the most time, utilise the most equipment, and aren't generally regarded as being suitable for novice fishkeepers.

The plus side is that there's nothing else quite like them, and the marine side of the hobby can also include keeping live corals and lots of specialised creatures that naturally associate with coral reefs.

WHAT YOU NEED TO KNOW ABOUT MARINE FISH

Water-changes take longer, as you need to prepare a special salt mix. Also, although thousands of fish can be found living together on reefs only a small proportion will mix in a marine aquarium, and most need lots of space. Nano aquariums are possible, in which a miniature and much less expensive reef environment can be created.

So, have a long, hard think about what type of fish you're going to opt for, and take a look at the chart below:

	Coldwater fish	Tropical fish	Marine fish
Choice of species	Low	High	High
Ease of keeping	Easy	Easy to difficult	Moderate to difficult
Start-up costs	Low	Low to high	High
Running costs	Low	Low to High	High

Choosing an aquarium

Though buying an aquarium is often the first thing people do when they're thinking about keeping fish, there are other decisions that should be made first so as to ensure that you choose a tank that suits not only your needs, but also the needs of your fish.

Aquariums come in a huge range of shapes and sizes, and though all are intended to hold water and fish some are more suitable than others. We want our aquariums to look good not only on the inside, but on the outside too. Nevertheless, although style is a factor it's the needs of the fish that must come first.

Shape

A tank must have a large surface area in relation to its volume, so that gases can pass freely through the surface of the water. Fish are also adapted to swim horizontally, so to do this they require a tank that's longer than it is tall, and one that's wide enough for them to turn around and then swim the other way.

The most practical shape for a fish tank is a rectangle, as it fulfils the requirements of the fish in terms of swimming space, and has a large surface area. Next are the bow-fronted tanks that are almost as suitable as rectangles. The curved front pane makes these tanks look good when decorated, and they're very popular.

Corner tanks are deep front to back, but may not be very long. They make for interesting aquascapes, as rock, corals or plants can be stacked up right into the rear corner, but they have less surface area in relation to their volume than bow-fronts or rectangles.

Cube tanks are compact, and popular because they don't have a large footprint, though this works against them in terms of surface area and swimming length.

Bowls and cylinders are the least suitable due to their small surface area and lack of swimming space.

Matching fish shape to tank shape

As a general rule, tall-bodied fish require tall tanks, so species such as Discus and Angelfish need a tank that's at least four times their body height so that they can move freely through the water. Slender-bodied fish like danios and guppies inhabit shallow water in their natural environment, so a shallow tank is best for them. Wide-bodied fish like stingrays require very wide aquariums front to back so that they can turn around easily, and have lots of space on the bottom to forage for food.

Size

When it comes to choosing a tank, bigger is better, as larger volumes of water are more stable in terms of water quality and temperature. And when you think about it, although an aquarium 1.2m long may seem large when placed in your living room, when compared to the rivers and lakes that our fish naturally swim in it's actually very small.

> **TIP**
>
> When choosing an aquarium, first choose the fish that you want to keep, and then find the most suitable tank that fulfils its needs.

As a very rough guide, a fish needs a tank at least six times its body-length long and twice its body-length wide in which to swim naturally and turn around. That means that a 15cm fish like a Blue Gourami needs an aquarium 0.9m in length, and 0.3m wide, and a 30cm Oscar needs an aquarium 1.8m long by 0.6m wide to be happy and to be able to exercise long-term.

Fish can and do grow to their maximum potential when kept in aquariums, so choose a tank that can house your chosen fish comfortably for their entire lives. Don't buy a small specimen of a big fish if you don't intend to increase the size of its accommodation proportionately as it grows, as unwanted large fish are common in the hobby, and zoos and public aquariums will *not* rehouse them for you.

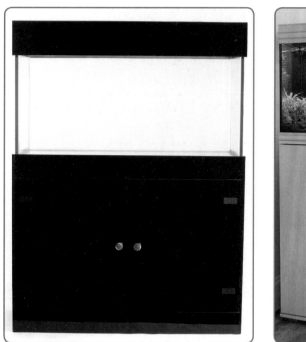

Once you've found a tank that's large enough to house your chosen species, you need to do further research to establish whether the fish are a solitary or a shoaling species and how active they are. A 5cm Tiger Barb wouldn't need a very large tank if it was kept on its own and wasn't very active, but since it lives in large shoals and is an active species a tank must be chosen to house not one but ten or more, plus other companions, which means a large tank.

Nano Aquariums

A nano aquarium is small aquarium, typically holding less than 100 litres of water, total volume. As long as there have been aquariums there have been small aquariums, only in modern times these small aquariums have been renamed nano aquariums.

A nano aquarium is also typically compact, being cubic in shape and with a small footprint, enabling placement on a desk or table. It will also often come with a built in hood, light and filter.

Nanos can be set up to hold coldwater, tropical or marine fish, though due to their small size, the livestock and décor choice must also be small sized. The idea is to create a fully functional, but miniature version of a larger aquarium, with live plants or corals, and a selection of a small fish, be they freshwater or marine.

Nanos have many advantages over larger aquariums as they are cheap to set up, cheap to maintain, they also use little electricity, and don't take up much space. That is why they are so popular. The downside however is that small bodies of water are less stable than large ones, meaning extra vigilance and care by the owner, and they can of course hold fewer fish. The author always recommends choosing as large a tank as possible, but if you simply don't have the space available to keep anything else, a nano aquarium is the practical solution.

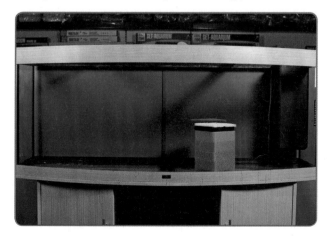

Aquarium placement

Once you've chosen the aquarium, it needs to be placed correctly. There are a whole lot of factors that affect where your tank should go.

Will it fit?

You will have had an idea of the size of the tank that you wanted before you bought it, but if you bought a very large tank of 2m or more, or over 0.6m wide, did you check that it

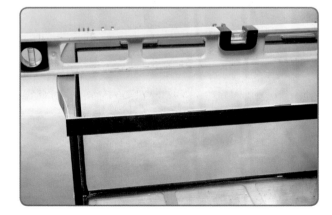

would even fit through the door? It sounds stupid, but it does happen, and if it won't go through and you won't give up your new tank, the windows may have to come out to get it in. So take a tape measure when choosing the tank, and it may pay off in the long run.

Where will it go?

In the average living room, some sites are better than others for placing your new aquarium. Fish frighten easily, so keep the tank away from doorways where people pass through, and draughts that could cool the water. Natural sunlight can also be bad if it falls on an aquarium, as it may heat up the water and encourage algae.

Fish are also very sensitive to noise and vibration, so the tank should be placed away from the television (it would compete for your viewing attention anyway), and definitely shouldn't be near any hi-fi speakers.

Place it in a position that's away from radiators, windows and doorways, but is level, near to electrical sockets and convenient for you to sit down and view it, such as opposite the sofa. A good-looking aquarium should take pride of place in any room.

Use a spirit level to check that the floor is level, as if it isn't the water will find its own level, and the waterline and the tank trim won't meet up.

How much will it weigh?

This is an important consideration, as when they're filled with water aquariums can be very heavy. A large community aquarium of, say, 1.2m x 45cm x 38cm will weigh 53.8kg empty, and 268.5kg full. This is a lot of weight, and when placing such a tank over floorboards it's wise to spread the weight horizontally over several joists. (Joists run the opposite way to the floorboards that sit on top of them.)

A tank of this size is about the limit that you could place upstairs on floorboards too, as even at that weight it's still about the same as a bathtub full of water. Any larger and you should consider taking advice from a structural engineer, as you may need a concrete or reinforced floor to support it.

Weight can be spread by using a cabinet instead of a stand with four small legs, and by removing the cabinet's feet.

Cushioning

Traditionally, glass aquariums should be placed on a layer of polystyrene to iron out any irregularities between the glass bottom and the top of the cabinet. Failure to do so could lead to the tank base cracking, causing a flood, and you'd pay the ultimate price of losing your livestock.

Some aquariums now come with their own base frame for cushioning, their own foam base-mat, or a 'floating base' that actually raises the base of the aquarium off the bottom of the tank.

TIP

Never move an aquarium once filled. Even a small aquarium won't have been designed to be moved when it's full. It will be extremely heavy, and even dragging it may seriously stress its structural integrity.

Cushioning a floating base with polystyrene could actually cause problems, so always check at the time of purchase whether it's a glass tank that needs to be cushioned, or has a floating base and shouldn't be cushioned. Failure to do so may void the aquarium's guarantee in the event of breakage.

Give yourself space

Don't squeeze a tank into a tight alcove, or right up against a wall, as you will usually need a small gap at the back for cables, a hang-on protein skimmer or filter pipe work. Leave yourself space to manoeuvre and maintenance will be easier too.

Safety first!

Electricity and water don't mix, so make sure that the tank is not placed directly over electrical sockets. Make sure that any cables have a simple drip loop – a sag in the cable so that if any water does run down it, it will collect at the bottom of the loop and then  drip off. If you stretch a cable diagonally down to a socket and any water gets on it, it will run straight into the power supply!

Residual current devices, or RCD circuit breakers, aren't just the domain of outdoor ponds, but will also provide an extra safety measure indoors if any equipment fails.

Essential equipment

Once an aquarium has been selected you must install the life support system for the fish, and buy the sundry necessary items that will keep them alive. Some aquariums and cabinets already come with heating, lighting and filtration, so all you need to do is decorate, fill with water, and plug in. The important part of maturing the tank is yet to come, however.

If putting together your own list of equipment, make sure you make the retailer aware of the make, model and size of your aquarium, so that you get the right equipment for it.

Shopping list

ESSENTIALS
- Aquarium
- Hood
- Cabinet
- Filter – to clear the water of debris and pollution
- Heater (if keeping tropical or marine fish) – to warm the water and keep it a constant temperature
- Fluorescent light tube – to illuminate the aquarium and show off the fishes' colours
- Light starter unit – to power the light tube
- Test kit – to monitor water quality
- Thermometer – essential to monitor water temperature
- Dechlorinator – to make tap water safe for fish
- Bacterial starter – to make your filter ready for fish
- Substrate
- Decor

MAINTENANCE EQUIPMENT
- Algae magnet or scraper
- Gravel vacuum
- Siphon tube
- Measuring jug
- Bucket

OPTIONAL
- Reflectors
- Condensation tray
- Aquarium background

Systemised, set-up, or build your own?

Buying an aquarium isn't like it used to be. You used to walk into the aquatic shop, choose the type of fish and size of tank that you wanted, and then buy all the accessories to go with it. These days many aquarium manufacturers have done the work of choosing the equipment for you, and some have even fitted them for you. A complete set-up is one where the tank, hood, lighting, filtration, heating and other items have been chosen for you and come with the tank at an all-in-one price. These set-ups can be useful for beginners, as you're usually safe in the knowledge that the manufacturer will have chosen the right size of heater and filter, for example, and there are usually other items like a food

Above: Systemised aquariums are very popular as the hard work of choosing the right kit has been done for you.

sample, maybe some water conditioners and a booklet. The advantage with set-ups is that they remove the risk of making mistakes if you build your own system, and when you buy it as an all-in-one bundle you get a saving on the total cost too.

Systemised

These are becoming more and more popular. A systemised aquarium is one that comes with a built-in hood, filter and lighting. Heaters are often included too. Systemised aquariums can be an even easier choice than a set-up, as not only has the correct equipment been chosen for you, but the light has been fitted, usually into a built-in housing; the filter has been built into the structure of the tank, so there's no risk of you fitting it wrongly; and most, if they come with a

heater, will even have it housed in a chamber next to the filter. Some systemised aquariums may even be all wired into one plug with a built-in light timer, so all you need do is decorate, fill up, plug in, and you're away. It's because of the ease of setting them up that systemised aquariums are so popular, and they're coming down in price all the time.

Build your own

But not everything in life is that simple, or solved by a systemised aquarium. If you want more lighting than normal, systemised aquariums can be limiting. If you want to fit, say, extra filtration they can be a pain too. Have a think about where your hobby is going to lead over the next year or so. A systemised aquarium or complete set-up is great for beginners, includes lots of essential kit and will house the majority of the fish available, but what if you want to specialise? If you keep and want to breed Siamese fighting fish, for example, you'll not require the power filtration that comes with a systemised aquarium.

When your hobby branches out it may be more cost-effective to build your own system by choosing equipment suited to your own special needs. Take advice from your retailer or experienced hobbyists on the equipment needed to breed fish etc, and who knows, if you buy it all in one go you may still get discount on it as a bulk purchase.

Left: Here the manufacturer has built a tank, hood and cabinet specifically to be fitted with an external filter.

Filtration

Filtration is the single most important function to get right in an aquarium, as it's the filtration that maintains the water quality. Without filtration, we would not have the hobby that we have today.

Why filter?

In nature, fish produce waste, but the bodies of water that they live in are so vast that the waste is diluted and washed away. A natural body of water will hold a finite number of

fish based on the amount of oxygen it holds, the food it produces, and the waste that it can dilute.

An aquarium is very different to a natural body of water, as it is a closed system. This means that unless we change and filter the water it will quickly become polluted with fish waste, and due to its small surface area it will run out of oxygen too. Because of these factors, an indoor aquarium left to its own devices would be unable to support any fish at all.

Not only do we place our fish into a closed system, but we also massively increase the stock density per cubic metre when compared to fish habitats in the wild. This means that if we want our fish to stay alive and healthy in our aquariums, we *must* break down or remove their waste and add oxygen. Filtration can do all three of these things, and makes keeping fish in captivity possible.

How a filter works

In its most basic form, a filter works mechanically, trapping waste particles suspended in the water, which we then remove. We can see mechanical filtration happening in front of our eyes, as in its most basic form a filter clears the water of debris, so that we can see our fish. Mechanical filtration is limited, though, as although it can remove solid waste it can't remove liquid pollutants from the water.

A biological filter can remove liquid waste (fish urine and ammonia) from the water, effectively clearing it of some organic pollutants. This is not so much the work of the filter itself but rather of the organisms that live inside it, since a biological filter is designed to create a home for beneficial bacteria which then break down and convert liquid pollutants. This job is vital in any aquarium, be it coldwater, tropical or marine, and the biological filter is the most important type of filter available because of its key role in making the

TIP

Filters must run for 24 hours per day if the beneficial bacteria are to be kept alive. Turn your filter off for more than a few minutes, replace the biological media, or wash the media under a tap and all the bacteria will be lost, causing 'new tank syndrome'. See pages 53.

water safe for fish to live in. To add beneficial bacteria, we carry out a process known as cycling, for which see pages 52–3.

Some filters can also work chemically, using substances that react in water to absorb chemicals from it. A chemical filter is usually used to remove one thing in particular, such as ammonia, nitrate, or even colouration in the water produced by adding bogwood or peat. Chemical media has a finite life, and must be replaced. For examples of mechanical, biological and chemical media, see pages 22–3.

What you need to know about filters

There are many different types of filter on the market, but the one thing that they all have in common is their vital role as a life-support system for your fish. The author does not recommend ever setting up or attempting to run an aquarium without some form of biological filtration. Daily water-

changes would need to be carried out in such a case, and water quality would not remain stable around feeding time.

Choosing a filter

The type of filter that you choose will depend on the type of fish you intend to keep, how many you intend to keep, and the size of the aquarium that they'll be living in. Small tanks only need small filters, and large tanks need large filters; but if you intend to overstock a small tank, or to keep fish that are messy eaters – such as goldfish – even a small tank may need two small filters or one larger one. Water-changes would need to be increased too.

It's not just how messy the fish are or the number there are in the tank, though, as filters differ in their output. Air-powered foam filters offer a gentle current, so will suit very small fish, fish fry, and fish that naturally inhabit still water. A still-water fish will not appreciate strong currents, and would become stressed if subjected to them long-term. Bettas and gouramies are classic examples of still-water fish.

But some fish do require strong water flow, which can be provided by a powerful filter. Riverine fish species (also known as reophilic fish) are adapted to live in strong, laminar water flow and their bodies are streamlined to cope with it. They also have a higher oxygen requirement, which would be part and parcel of a fast-flowing river. A power filter would be the obvious choice for such species.

But regardless of whether your fish would naturally inhabit fast or still water, mechanical and biological filters must always be present in the aquarium, and the bigger the biological filter the better, as it will cope with more waste.

Internal power filters

These are the most common form of filtration available, as they are compact, reliable and affordable. Typically an internal filter consists of a sponge in a canister, with a powerhead on top.

How they work
In simple terms, water is drawn in through slots in the canister, waste is trapped in the sponge, and the water is pumped out through the top by the powerhead. After a time the sponge will start to become effective biologically as bacteria take up residence on it.

What's good about them?
Because of their simple design internal filters are suitable for beginners and experts alike, and will often filter and aerate the water at the same time. They're easy to maintain and are durable.

What's not so good?
Their affordable price and compact size does sometimes mean a compromise when it comes to media capacity, and if you keep lots of fish – or messy fish – you'll either need several or, better still, you'll need to upgrade to an external filter.

Choosing a model
Internal filters will be rated for a certain volume of water, or tank length, and as the models get larger they contain more media and have a more powerful output.

Although they don't generally contain much media when compared to an external filter, some makes and models have more than others. Choose a model with two sponges, so that one can be cleaned or replaced while the other is left in place to continue harbouring the essential bacteria.

A top-of-the-range internal filter should contain a number of features for your convenience. Additional media may be supplied, including dedicated ceramic media for biological filtering, and chemical media such as carbon to purify the water.

TIP
Never replace all your filter media at once, as beneficial bacteria will be lost. Either cut the mature sponge in half and replace just half at a time, or, if multiple media are supplied, leave the biological media in place to take care of the breakdown of waste. Never wash filter media under the tap, as the chlorine will kill the beneficial bacteria.

Directional flow control is an added bonus, as is an output adjuster so that the flow can be turned up or down. The icing on the cake is an optional venturi, to provide aeration as well as filtration.

MULTI-CHAMBER INTERNAL FILTERS
These large 'box' filters have several types of media and a large capacity like an external filter; only they fit inside the aquarium. Box filters often have a chamber inside to take a heater, keeping it out of harm's way, and the large amount of media means that a proportion can always be changed or cleaned without having to worry about bacteria levels. Some fix permanently to the inside of the tank with silicone, and are a good compromise for those who wish to take advantage of the internal and external filters' key features.

External power filters

Externals are the best form of filtration available off the shelf in aquarium stores. They're larger and more powerful than internal filters, and contain more media. Instead of fitting inside the aquarium, externals are designed to be placed beneath the tank and connect to it via pipe work – an inlet pipe and an outlet pipe. This has advantages in that the filter body can be maintained without disturbing the fish, and no bulky equipment is on show in the tank above.

External filters really come into their own when filtering aquariums of over 200 litres' capacity or 0.9m length. Because of their large size they easily cope with large numbers of fish, messy fish, and very large fish, and rarely block or clog up.

Choosing a model
Choose an external filter that's equipped to take a variety of different media including sponge, ceramic, biological and chemical. If all media are supplied as part of the package, so much the better, but the versatility of an external filter means that it should be able to take

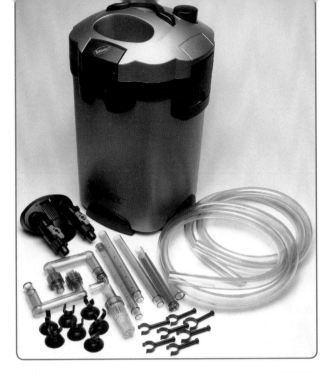

whatever media you choose, from peat to filter wool to large plastic media. And the media can be arranged as you require.

All pipe work should come supplied and typically contains an inlet strainer to stop fish being sucked in, and a number of outlets including a spray bar to return and oxygenate the water.

Some external filters come with a priming mechanism, meaning they have an inbuilt device that enables you to fill the canister with water from the main tank automatically, instead of having to fill it with a jug or siphon. Priming mechanisms are convenient and save time, and should prevent you from having to get your hands wet – which is well worth considering when buying a filter.

Jargon buster

Venturi A device that fits to the outlet of a power filter, sucking in air and blowing fine bubbles into the water.

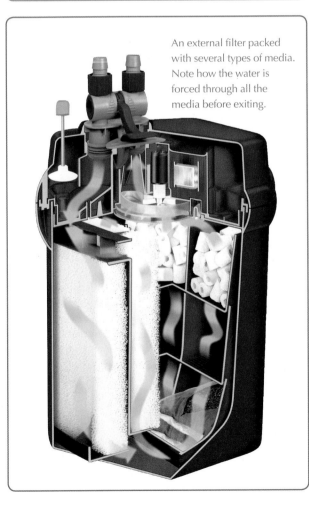

An external filter packed with several types of media. Note how the water is forced through all the media before exiting.

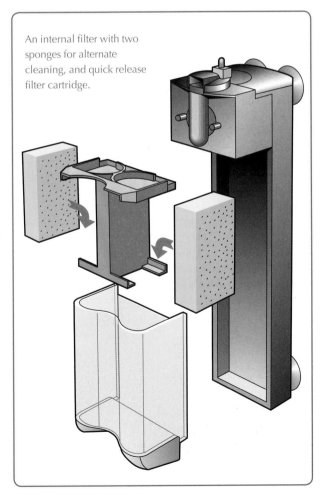

An internal filter with two sponges for alternate cleaning, and quick release filter cartridge.

Filter media

Mechanical media

This is the most basic form of filtration, and one that the fishkeeper can actually see working. Put simply, mechanical filtration removes particles from the water by trapping them as they flow past.

Some form of mechanical filtration is vital in coldwater and tropical aquariums as its helps to keep the water free of debris, and aids water clarity, so that you can see your fish. Mechanical media is normally made up of sponge or filter wool, also known as filter floss. This is of white polyester, either in a big clump for you to fit to size or in a pre-cut size to fit your make and model of filter.

Filter wool traps large and fine particles, and is so effective at trapping waste that it can clog up quite quickly. It

can be washed to remove debris and reused, though due to its cheap cost it is usually thrown away and renewed on a weekly basis. Filter wool is mechanical only, and should not be used on its own to support fish.

Probably the most common mechanical filter media is sponge, also known as foam. It comes in a variety of densities from very fine to very coarse, and the density will determine what size particles it will trap, how quickly it will clog, and the water turnover per hour that you can put through it.

Sponge does clog, but it can be washed and reused for months afterwards. When it starts to lose its shape and not spring back after being squeezed it should be removed and replaced. Because of its structure, sponge can also become a home for beneficial bacteria, filtering both mechanically and

biologically. It's because of these dual benefits that small filters or expensive filters often come with just one piece of sponge to do all the filtering. The low cost is a benefit, but if the sponge becomes clogged it will lose its biological filtering capacity, and if you wash it or replace it bacteria will be lost and your fish could be in trouble. It's therefore much better to use it in conjunction with other media.

Biological media

Apart from sponge, biological media come in all different shapes and sizes. Unlike mechanical media its job is not to trap particles and clear the water. Instead, it's designed to specifically house live bacteria on its surface and within it. Good biological media will have a huge surface area in relation to its size, something that's usually achieved by making the outside surfaces very irregular and by giving it a porous internal structure.

Ceramic media is the most popular choice, be it natural or man-made, as it has both a large surface area and a porous interior. Ceramic media can take the form of rough rock chippings, circular hoops, balls, and anything that makes a good home for bacteria.

Plastic can also be used to manufacture a large surface area media for bacteria. These generally have very intricate shapes, and are used in quantity either in a separate filter area to ceramic media, or instead of ceramics in tanks or ponds with high filter turnover.

Chemical media

Chemical media perform those tasks that mechanical or biological media can't. Depending on what it is, a chemical media can remove things from the water and lock them away, unlike bacteria that break down organics and convert them. When the substance has been absorbed, or the chemical media is spent, you throw it away.

> **TIP**
>
> Remember never to wash biological media under the tap. Beneficial bacteria will be killed and washed away by the chlorine and chloramines in tap water.

Carbon is the most popular form of chemical filtration by far, and is inexpensive. Also known as charcoal, carbon can clear water by removing dyes, pigments, stains, odours and even medications. It's commonly used to remove the tannins released by bogwood and to make the water look as clean and as clear as possible. Carbon comes in standard or activated forms, the latter being more porous and having a higher surface area, which makes it better at absorbing. Carbon should be thrown away and replaced every four weeks, or if you don't feel you need it to remove any dyes, odours or medications you can do without it all together.

Zeolite is a chemical media that can remove ammonia from aquarium water. This makes it a useful short-term fix if you're registering dangerous levels of ammonia on your test kit, or if you're moving fish over long distances and they're at risk of polluting their own water. Once used it can be thrown away. In the author's view Zeolite shouldn't be used in a filtered aquarium unless you have to, as the removal of an ammonia source for beneficial bacteria means that the colony will shrink in size and not be ready for ammonia the next time. It's useful for emergencies, though.

Heating

In the cooler parts of the world, heating is essential if you wish to keep tropical fish. The fish that we keep in aquariums naturally inhabit warm waters in South and Central America, South-East Asia, Africa and Australasia, and enjoy year round temperatures between 20° and 30°C.

If your living space and tap water doesn't provide these same constant temperatures, then you must provide artificial means to heat the water and keep the fish happy.

Heater thermostats

These are by far the most common pieces of equipment used to heat aquariums, and consist of a thermostat connected to a heating element and placed in a waterproof tube. Heater thermostats plug in to the mains electricity and once set to the desired temperature and placed underwater they'll turn themselves on and off to regulate the heat.

Turning a small knob on the top of the heater normally sets the temperature, and some models have a display that indicates the temperature you've set it to. Most heaters are sealed inside a cylindrical glass tube, which enables good heat transfer, although the nature of the glass casing means that care must be taken not to shatter it.

How heaters work

Traditionally, heater thermostats work by way of a bi-metallic strip. The strip is made up of two pieces of metal fastened together, one steel and one copper. The two expand at different rates when exposed to heat, causing the strip to bend. One strip is connected to a power source, the other to an electrical connection. When heated sufficiently the connection is broken, and when it cools the connection is re-established.

A more modern way – and, some would say, a more reliable way – is to control heating in a thermostat by microchip. This method remains more expensive than bi-metallic strips, which is usually reflected in the price of the heater.

Recent developments include heaters made from tough, unbreakable materials for much greater durability; heaters that just heat an element to the required water temperature, making it safe to handle; and heaters that also display the actual temperature of the water on a digital display, as opposed to just showing the temperature that the device is set to. This

Below: A combined heater/thermostat is needed to regulate temperature in a tropical aquarium. This model comes with a protective guard, too.

enables more accurate monitoring of the water temperature and will quickly alert you if something has gone wrong.

Other types of heater

A less common form of heating these days is the separate heater and thermostat. With this method, heater and thermostat are bought separately and then connected manually with wiring. There can be advantages to this method, as the thermostat can be located outside of the aquarium and can be close to hand for ease of temperature adjustment. An external thermostat reads the water temperature with a probe.

Separate thermostats can also control much larger capacity heaters, such as 600W for example, or two smaller heaters at the same time. They also mean that your selected heater can be of any shape, quality and output. Care should be taken when choosing a heater/thermostat, though, as a low-quality heater may fail, and if this happens with a tank full of marine livestock it can be very costly. Would you leave marine livestock equal in value to a second-hand car at the mercy of a heater of the same value as a music CD?

Titanium heaters are available, and could be the best choice in terms of reliability and build quality.

In-line heaters

An in-line heater is a heater/thermostat that connects to external filter pipe work, instead of going in the main tank. Advantages are that the device won't burn the fish; it remains hidden away instead of becoming an eyesore in the main tank; and its temperature can be adjusted without

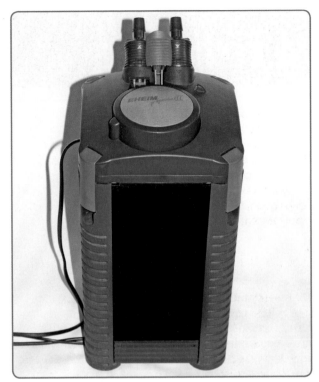

Above left: In-line heaters connect to external filter pipe work, hidden away from view.

Above: Thermo filters have a heater/thermostat built into the canister, for even heat distribution.

Right: A thermometer is an essential piece of kit for any aquarium.

getting your hands wet. Some models even turn themselves off if the water flow stops. Another advantage is that the water flow distributes the heat evenly throughout the aquarium.

External filters are also available with a built-in heating element and thermostat. They share many features with in-line heaters in that heat is distributed evenly, the heater is kept out of the main tank for better aesthetics, and the fish can't get to it. 'Thermofilters' are available for both freshwater and saltwater aquariums.

TIP

Never take a glass heater out of the water when it's on, or within ten minutes of it having been on. The glass will shatter! If you need to remove a heater, think ahead, and unplug it for 30 minutes before you remove it from the water.

TIP

To protect heaters from knocks and breakages, fit a heater guard. These plastic protectors slide over the heater body, preventing damage while still allowing heat through.

Lighting

Lighting is essential for all aquarium creatures. We use it both to see them, and to replicate the sun streaming through clear water. There are lots of artificial forms of lighting to choose from, and it's important to choose the one that's right for the aquarium's inhabitants and for you.

T8

At the time of writing T8 is still the most popular form of aquarium lighting, with the most sizes, colours and spectrums available. The term 'T8' derives from the fact that they're 8/8ths of an inch, or 1in, in diameter. Selected models are available with built-in reflectors, though clip-on reflectors are better.

An aquarium fitted with one T8 light tube would be considered low or standard lighting, and if growing plants or keeping an aquarium that's 38cm deep or deeper several T8 tubes would be needed. A typical marine aquarium with corals would require at least four T8 tubes with reflectors, so most marine keepers choose T5 instead.

T5

The brightest fluorescent lighting available, T5 is so-named from being 5/8ths of an inch in diameter. In general, T5 emits more light by length than T8, but it does it by consuming more electricity too. T5 must be run using a T5 lighting ballast.

Linear T5

Linear T5 is a long, thin, double-ended tube that connects to a lamp-holder at each end. It ranges in size from 30cm to about 1.5m and is available in a huge range of colour outputs. Two linear T5s with reflectors would be adequate to grow plants and some corals in most aquarium depths. Four linear T5s plus reflectors would be considered high light and could provide bright lighting for tanks up to 0.6m deep.

PCT5

Power compact T5 looks like a linear T5 that's been doubled over on itself, and it has only one end to connect to a lamp-holder. It comes in a range of sizes, colours and spectrums and can be very small and short, down to just a few centimetres in length.

Although compact, PCT5s emit a lot of light in a small space, and they're popular for nano aquariums with demanding species of corals or plants. The downside is that  because they're doubled over and quite wide, they aren't as efficient as a linear T5 when used with a reflector. One PCT5 could provide enough light for most small tanks, with two being considered medium light and four providing high levels of light in most aquariums up to 0.6m deep.

T12

T12 was the predecessor of T8, and was the first form of fluorescent lighting used in the aquatics market. They're largely obsolete these days and offer no advantages, as T8 and T5 are available in more spectrums and emit more light per watt.

T6

T6 is relatively new and falls between T8 and T5 in terms of both diameter and brightness. The advantage of T6 is that, with adaptors fitted, it can be used in T8 lamp-holders.

Metal halide

Metal halide lamps are also known as Hi Intensity Discharge (HID) lamps, and run at high pressure and high temperature. Because of their temperature they shouldn't be mounted inside the hood of an aquarium, and instead come in a special housing which is then suspended above the tank.

Metal halides are point source lights, meaning that you get a very 'spotlight' effect that looks like sunlight shining through the water. This effect is very desirable, and their ability to penetrate water means that they're often the only choice for demanding species of corals or plants in aquariums over 0.6m in depth.

Bulbs come in 70W, 150W, 250W, 400W and even 1,000W sizes. One 150W bulb will provide very bright lighting for an aquarium of 90cm length, and larger sizes are usually only used for huge display aquariums or very demanding coral species that need strong lighting to replicate the midday tropical sun. Some metal halides come in combination with T8 or T5 tubes for even greater lighting effects and spectral range. The extra lighting can also be timed to come on before and go off after the metal halides, to provide a dawn and dusk effect.

LED

LED lighting has many advantages to the modern fishkeeper. It's very bright, can come in any imaginable colour and doesn't use much electricity. It also doesn't need reflectors, using small lenses instead, and emits low levels of heat compared to other forms of lighting. It can even be dimmed electronically. It's also said that LEDs are a greener form of lighting because each of them can emit light for a period of around ten years and they have low energy requirements.

They also don't contain mercury, so aren't classed as hazardous waste when they're disposed of. Most LED units are completely waterproof too.

Feature lighting

Not to be confused with the lighting that you use to illuminate the main tank, or to benefit plants or corals, feature lighting is intended purely to provide effects, such as to light the inside of a cave ornament or provide a beam of coloured light through a stream of bubbles. Although they don't provide natural light, the fish don't actually mind them, and they can be used for effect in ornamental-looking aquariums.

Reflectors

You can increase the output of any fluorescent tube by fitting reflectors. Usually matt white or polished aluminium, these clip on to the light tube and direct all the light down

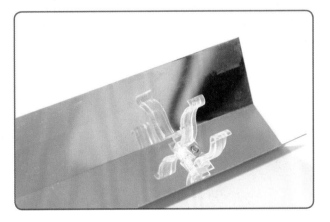

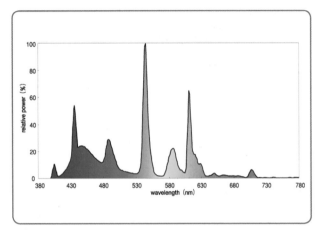

Above: A daylight tube.

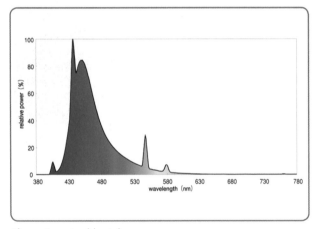

Above: A marine blue tube.
Below: A colour enhancing tube.

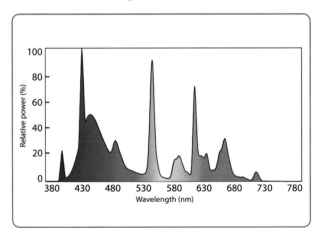

into the aquarium. They also shield your eyes when you open the hood.

Depending on the design of the tube, and the design of the reflector, there can be something called 'restrike', where reflected light is wasted by hitting the tube directly from above. To counteract this, the best light tube to use with a reflector is a linear T5, as it's thin and doesn't offer much surface area for restrike. The best reflector design to eliminate restrike is one that looks like seagull wings in profile. This gull-wing shape directs light away from the top of the tube.

Spectrums

With so many lights available to the hobbyist it's hard to know which to choose, but they basically divide into two types: those that are aimed at lighting marine tanks, and those that are aimed at lighting freshwater.

In nature, sunlight delivers a full spectrum of colours as it penetrates water, though different parts of that spectrum are filtered out. In fresh, shallow water most of the sunlight penetrates, so aquatic plants have adapted to use the full spectrum which, when measured in colour temperature, or Kelvin rating, is 5,500K. Use this colour temperature over an aquarium and the light will look yellow/white. If the water is stained with tannins from wood and leaves some of the blue spectrum will be filtered out, so sunlight measured in tannin-stained water may be as low as 2,000K, which when used in aquariums looks quite orange.

When sunlight shines through seawater, however, the depth has a significant effect on it. As it shines down through metres of water, red, orange and yellow light are the first to be filtered out, leaving the blue spectrum dominant. The deeper the water gets, the more blue the

Below: An all-round tube will have peaks across the spectrum.

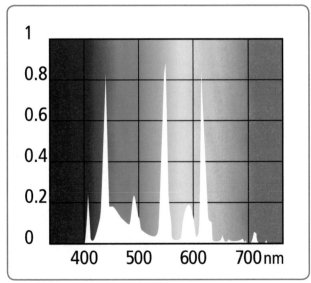

light gets and the higher the colour
temperature.

A marine white light will simulate
sunlight in just a few metres of water,
which will still look quite white and will
have a Kelvin rating between 10,000
and 14,000K. To simulate deep
seawater on a reef use 20,000K
lighting, and for greater depth, dawn,
dusk and even moonlight, use pure
blue light only – called actinic light –
which doesn't normally carry a Kelvin
rating, but when it does it will be
around 50,000K.

You can't accurately read Kelvin
ratings with the naked eye, but an
experienced fishkeeper can usually
guess it by whether the light looks
yellow, white, blue/white or blue.
Fortunately, lighting manufacturers
often offer the Kelvin rating and a
spectral graph on the packaging of
their products.

Duration

How long your lighting needs to stay on
for depends on the livestock that you
have in your tank. In a tank with just fish, replica rocks and
ornaments, and either replica plants or no live plants, you only
need the light on to view the fish. Four hours per day doesn't
seem like much, but the fish don't need any artificial light at
all and are fine in just ambient room light. Only have the light
on when you're viewing the fish, and the lack of light will
mean no build-up of nuisance algae.

If you have plants in freshwater, or corals in a marine
tank, they'll have adapted to take advantage of tropical
sunlight duration, typically ten to twelve hours per day. Any
more than that and they can't use it for growth, but algae
can, so keep the lighting on a strict daily regime by means
of a timer.

Lifespan

Lighting is bright and contains the necessary spectrum and
output when you buy it, but over time it starts to degrade.
You must therefore replace your lighting with new every
12 months.

What else do I need?

Fluorescent lighting tubes must be powered by a control
unit. This enables them to be connected to the mains in
order to work, and allows you to turn them on and off.

To stop light tubes from falling into the water, use clips,
which then fasten to both a reflector and the inside of the
hood of your aquarium. Systemised aquariums often come
with built-in lighting, containing the light tubes, the
controller and the on/off switch.

Jargon buster

HO High output.
VHO Very high output.

Aeration

Above: An air pump is a useful and inexpensive piece of equipment, which aerates the water.

Above: Submersible air pumps sit inside the aquarium, and draw in air through a tube.

Oxygen is vital for all aquatic organisms, and it's introduced into aquarium water in a number of ways.

Air pumps

The most common form of aeration in aquariums is via an air pump. Air pumps usually sit outside the aquarium, and plug into the mains. They work by way of a vibrating rubber diaphragm. As the diaphragm inside the pump vibrates, air is sucked in from the atmosphere and pumped into the aquarium at pressure via thin rubber tubing.

Surprisingly, it's not so much the bubbles going into the water that aerates it, but rather the surface agitation that the bubbles create as they break the surface. To create even more bubbles, and less noise, the airline (the tubing) is

Below: Air stones connect to an air pump via narrow airline, and release a fine stream of bubbles when underwater.

usually connected to a small, porous block called an airstone. Since the stream of fine bubbles that airstones create is pleasing to the eye, as well as benefiting the whole system, they're understandably popular, and airstones and pumps consequently come in sizes and styles to suit every type of aquarium.

Most air pumps should always be placed outside of the water, though some models are now designed to work inside the aquarium, and instead of pumping air in they suck it in via a pump and venturi under the water. Submersible air pumps may also come with colourful LED lighting for extra effect.

When to use an air pump

Although not every system needs additional aeration, air pumps benefit almost every type of aquarium and pond. The fish use up oxygen, so by adding extra oxygen they won't go short, and shouldn't ever suffocate. Some fish, such as coldwater species, have higher oxygen demands than others. Cold water naturally holds more oxygen than warm water, though when kept in our temperate, room-temperature aquariums even coldwater fish may suffer, so all coldwater aquariums benefit greatly from extra air.

Some tropical fish naturally inhabit well-oxygenated water, such as fast-flowing streams or at the bottom of waterfalls. Again, add extra air and the fish will be a lot better for it. Overcrowded aquariums will definitely need extra aeration, as the surface area will not allow enough air to diffuse naturally compared with the number of fish. Filters even need aeration, as filter bacteria are aerobic, meaning that they need oxygen. Add extra air, and your biological filter could perform better.

Using air with sick fish

An air pump and airstone are essential equipment for those who wish to treat sick fish. If a fish is ill, its breathing will be laboured, and if it is has a parasitic infection – such as Whitespot, for example – the parasite may be inside the gills, further hindering breathing.

Medications strip oxygen from the water, so always add extra aeration if you're treating sick fish. Air can help with water quality problems too, so aerate if ammonia or nitrite is found to be present, which will enable the filter bacteria to recover more quickly.

Non-return valves

When using an external air pump, you should always fit a simple but effective non-return valve. Its purpose is to allow air to pass through it freely on its way from the pump to the aquarium, and, if the air supply stops, to prevent any aquarium water from flowing back the opposite way.

If water gets into the pump it will ruin it, and it will have to be thrown away. There's also a real risk of electrocution,

as the pump will be plugged into the mains. Every pump (apart from those that are designed to be used underwater) must be connected to a non-return valve.

Aeration shopping list

■ Air pump rated for your size of aquarium.
■ Airline – enough to reach from the pump in the cabinet to the base of the aquarium, plus a bit more just in case.
■ Non-return valve – essential if the pump is to be placed below the waterline.
■ Airstone – any size and style will do, but big airstones need to be powered by big air pumps.
■ Air control tap – to regulate flow.
■ Clips and suckers – to fasten the pump and airline and stop them from floating.

Other ways to aerate

Venturi attachments on power filter outlets suck in air, and shoot fine bubbles into the water. This free form of aeration comes as an added bonus with most filters, though if the filter stops you'll lose the filtration and aeration in the tank, and your fish could be in trouble. If you keep species that are demanding of oxygen, a separate air pump is the better option.

Aquatic plants produce oxygen in the daytime, and this is enough for fish in most cases, though they do the opposite at night and consume it instead. A planted aquarium must be set up slightly differently in most cases, to accommodate both fish and plants. Surface agitation should suffice in most cases, and this can be achieved by placing the filter above, on, or just under the surface of the water, so that ripples are created.

Test kits

Test kits are absolutely vital if you keep fish. Crystal clear water could be free of pollutants, but it could also be lethal to fish, and the only way that we can get an indication of this is by testing the water.

Test kits allow us to check that pollutant levels aren't running too high, and if they are will show that we need to take action against them. They also indicate the chemistry of the water, such as whether it's acid or alkaline (which is essential for the well-being of some species). In fact the importance of test kits cannot be overemphasized, and can be the difference between a fishkeeper who thinks that they're doing it right but is making fundamental mistakes, and one who knows that everything's exactly as it should be and is getting much more satisfaction from the hobby.

When to test

If ever there's a problem in the tank, such as a fish looking ill, an experienced fishkeeper will always reach for the test kit first, as it will indicate whether or not the quality of the water is to blame. Note that 90 per cent of problems in aquariums are related to water quality.

If you're setting up a new aquarium, or are totally new to fishkeeping, the water should be tested weekly. But if your tests should ever indicate a water-quality issue, such as high levels of ammonia or nitrite, it should be tested daily. The results should be recorded and daily testing should continue until the problem has been sorted out and has gone away.

Good aquatic shops test water all the time, both for themselves and their customers, so it's helpful to be able to speak in the same fishy language and tell them the results of your own water-quality tests. If you can tell an expert what your water tests at, they'll be able to tell you if it's fine, if there's a problem, and if it's ready to take more fish.

Regular testing allows you to know your aquarium and how it works intimately. Over time you'll come to know when to change the water, how much to change in order to lower, say, levels of nitrate, and what the pH (acidity or alkalinity) values are, which will allow you to choose your fish more wisely by matching them to the pH of your tank. Once the tank is mature, monthly water tests will be fine.

TIP

Test kits go out of date, so always check that they're in date before testing. Some tests can be harmful if they come into contact with skin or eyes. Always follow the safety instructions on the packaging.

Types of test kit

The test kits available from aquatic shops come in several forms. The three most popular are dip strips, tablets and liquid test kits.

Dip strips

These are the quickest and most convenient form of test, though not necessarily the most accurate. A dip strip consists of a narrow plastic strip with indicator paper fixed to it. The strip is dipped in the tank water for a second or two, taken out while it changes colour, and then the colour is matched to a chart on the packaging.

Most dip strips can test for just one parameter, such as nitrite, but some combine several tests on one strip for a cross-section of at-a-glance results. Typical such combined test strips include pH, nitrite, nitrate, KH and GH (see panel), though you should find out whether they also test for ammonia, as not all of them do. If they don't, a separate ammonia test will need to be purchased. The strips are thrown away after being used once, and typically come in packs of 25 or 50.

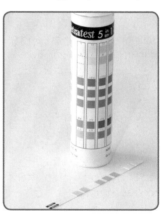

Left: Dip strips are quick, safe and easy to use.

Below: Tablet test kits are good for beginners, and test across the range of water parameters.

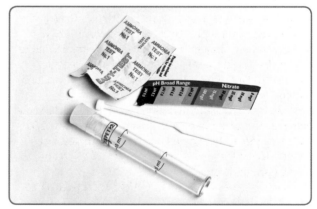

What am I testing for?

There are several water parameters that we commonly test for:

pH	How acid or alkaline the water is. Important when matching your water chemistry to what the fish naturally inhabit in the wild. Discus naturally inhabit water with low pH, whereas Mollies naturally inhabit water with a high pH. Get pH right, and your fish will feel more at home.
Ammonia	A deadly toxin released by fish as they urinate and breathe. Although they release it into the water, they are intolerant of it, so it must be removed by a biological filter. Test for ammonia at the first sign of fish ill health.
Nitrite	Bacteria produce nitrite as they consume and convert ammonia. It too is very toxic to fish so must be converted down further by a biological filter into nitrate. Test at the fist sign of ill health or when cycling a new aquarium.
Nitrate	The end product of converting ammonia and nitrite. Much less toxic than ammonia and nitrite though can be harmful to fish if allowed to build up to high levels. Reduce nitrate by changing water.
GH	General hardness, which is a measurement of the mineral content of water. Hard water will usually have a high pH, soft water will have a low pH, so the two are related.
KH	Carbonate hardness, which is a measurement of how much carbon dioxide is in water. Low KH is better for plant growth.
Phosphate	a natural plant fertiliser, though if not taken up by plants will fuel algae growth. It is also harmful to corals in marine tanks.

Tablets

Tablet tests come with a test tube and a colour chart, and typically contain tests for pH, ammonia, nitrite and nitrate. Fill the test tube up to the mark with aquarium water, drop the tablet in, crush it up or shake until it dissolves, and then cross-reference the colour with the chart. Tablet test kits can be used by fishkeepers of all skill levels, though they're best kept out of reach of young children. They typically come either as single tests, such as for pH for example, in which case they come in multiples of 20, or else they combine pH, ammonia, nitrite and nitrate tests in a master test kit. They're generally regarded as accurate.

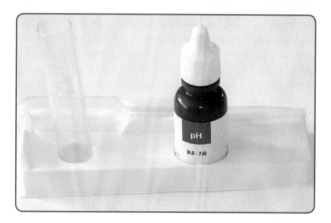

Liquid tests

Liquid tests are regarded as the most accurate. The liquid is added to a test tube filled with aquarium water, which is shaken, and the resultant colour is then cross-referenced to a chart. The liquid typically contains several reagents for one test, and a specific number of drops need to be added for the results to be accurate.

Liquid tests check for most things, including all the usual ones plus KH, GH, phosphate, calcium, iron, oxygen, CO_2 and many more. They come singly or in master test kits, but because of the chemicals they contain shouldn't be used by young children.

Liquid tests are both accurate and good value, as some kits will test 100 or more times.

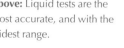

Above: Liquid tests are the most accurate, and with the widest range.

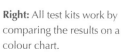

Right: All test kits work by comparing the results on a colour chart.

Substrates

A home aquarium needs something on the bottom for plants to anchor in, for fish to sift, and to make the tank look good. These are called substrates, and there are a number of different types to choose from.

Pea gravel

Pea gravel is a washed, smooth, inert (*ie* chemically inactive) gravel that's easy to keep clean by vacuuming and is suitable for medium to large fish that like to dig. Its shapes and colours provide a fresh, clean look to any freshwater aquarium, or a stream or river biotope aquarium. Typically available in 5–10mm grain sizes.

Silver sand

Silver sand also goes by many other names, but it basically looks like what you'd expect to find on beaches round the world or in a children's sandbox. It's very fine and will need to be washed before being placed in an aquarium.

Silver sand occurs naturally in freshwater and saltwater environments and many species of fish are adapted to sift through it to find food, including stingrays, Corydoras catfish and Geophagus cichlids.

It's soft and light in colour, though too dense to be used on its own with plants, and can compact if it's used in layers over 5cm deep. If used with very large fish and very large filters it can get sucked up into the filter system.

River sand

River sand can be fine like silver sand, or come in a mixture of grain sizes and shapes, and in brown, grey or golden colours. It's inert but will need washing, and is perfect for plants to anchor in and spread their roots through. River sand can be used for any freshwater set-up, but looks particularly good in well-decorated tanks and biotopes, where it forms a neutral bottom that enhances fish and plant colours.

Silica grit

Silica grit is orange in colour and typically comes in 1–3mm grain sizes. It's inert, and is actually used more frequently in swimming pool filters and commercial water purification systems as a mechanical filter. It can be used to effect in all types of freshwater aquarium, and when combined with a substrate fertiliser is a good substrate for plants.

Coloured gravel

Coloured gravels are inert natural grits and gravels covered with a fish-safe painted coating. They're available in everything from black to blue, bright pink, orange and white and everything in between. Mixtures containing several colours are very popular, and fluorescent shades are also available.

Coloured gravels are popular with first-time fishkeepers and those who want to add colour to their aquariums. The fish aren't too bothered, though light shades of gravel may actually 'wash out' the appearance of fish colours, and a brown catfish that likes to use its camouflage won't appreciate being offered a fluorescent pink substrate to try and blend in to. Smaller grain sizes are better for plants.

Coral sand

As its name suggests, this is a marine substrate made up of tiny coral fragments. It's most often only found in saltwater aquariums, though its pH and alkalinity-buffering properties can be put to good use in freshwater, hard water aquariums such as Lake Malawi cichlid tanks.

Due to its colour and texture it does provide a 'marine look' in freshwater, especially when combined with either ocean rock or tufa, though it must not be used with soft water species because of how it alters and raises the pH. This also makes it unsuitable for planted aquariums.

Baked clay

Baked clay consists of clay granules baked at very high temperatures, which causes them to become porous and light. It's therefore much lighter than normal sand or gravel. There are several types available, usually marketed for use in planted aquariums since they're said to still be able to release beneficial minerals that aid plant growth.

Normally red or brown, baked clay can also be the colour of ashes. Being inert, it can be used on its own in a freshwater aquarium, or else on its own or combined with substrate fertilisers in a planted aquarium. It provides a uniform but natural look.

Freshwater décor

Rocks

Slate

Slate is a dark, smooth rock, but with sharp edges. Typically available in flat sheets, it can be used for stacking

and to construct small bridges to span gaps. It can be split and broken easily with a hammer, and is inert and therefore suitable for any freshwater aquarium.

Cobbles

Cobbles are medium to large smooth rocks that are inert and suitable for al freshwater aquariums. Large cobbles are typical of stream, river and Lake Malawi set-ups. They're very dense and heavy and don't stack very well, so should only be used one layer high in most cases. The smooth edges make them suitable for clumsy species such as fancy goldfish.

Ocean rock

Ocean rock is a calcareous rock originally formed in the sea. Being calcareous it's only safe for marine fish and hard water, freshwater fish. Its bright colours and stark shapes can be

used to create a very architectural aquascape, or it can be used as a base rock on top of which other more expensive rocks are placed. It can also be stacked, but it's very heavy so measures must be taken to ensure that it doesn't fall and crack the tank glass.

Tufa

Tufa is a crumbly calcareous rock that's only suitable for hard water, freshwater tanks or marine tanks. It's bright in colour and is so soft that it can be drilled at home in order to create holes and caves. It can be stacked, and when used in

combination with coral sand can provide a marine look to freshwater tanks. It isn't used so much these days, as some authorities believe that it can trap and then release nitrates into the water.

Lava

Lava rock comes from volcanoes, is light, and has an interesting texture. Available either with holes carved in it or as lumps, it can be stacked high without difficulty and is so

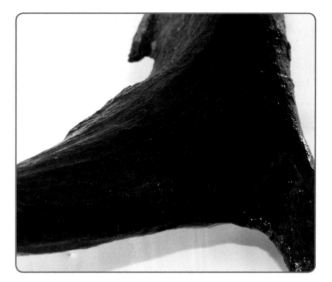

light that even if it did fall over, it would rarely cause any damage. Lava is inert and suitable for any set up, though its rough surfaces aren't ideal for algae grazing fish or clumsy fancy goldfish. Check that it sinks before you buy it, as some lava is so light and full of air that it actually floats!

Petrified wood

Petrified wood is timber that has fossilised into rock over the millennia. It's inert and appealing to the eye, and can be used in all freshwater situations from coldwater aquariums to cichlid tanks to planted tanks. It's quite heavy, but the more of it you use the better it looks.

Wood

Bogwood

Bogwood is a catch-all name these days for any wood used in aquariums, and rarely comes from bogs. It must sink, and be safe to use with fish, so only use bogwood available from aquatic shops.

Bogwood comes from all over the world and in many different sizes and textures. It can range from large, heavy chunks to more intricate branching pieces, and is very popular for setting a natural scene in tropical aquariums. It tends to leach tannins into the water, which stain it brown. This is normal, and many fish inhabit tannin-stained water in the wild, but if you don't wish to have brown water in your tank use carbon to remove the stain, or else soak the wood for several weeks before you use it. It's

always wise to soak wood anyway before placing it in an aquarium.

Branches and leaves

For a dramatic, wild effect, leaves and branches can be used. Again this happens all the time in the wild, and many catfish in particular are camouflaged to look like tree bark or leaves. Combine it with fine sand for an authentic Amazonian biotope look.

However, there's a catch with using leaves and twigs – they break down and decay in the water, and may become fungused. For this reason they're not recommended for many situations or for beginners, and plenty of water-changes combined with hefty filtration should be used to counteract the decaying process. Don't use just any leaves either, as some are poisonous. If in doubt, the leaves from beech and oak trees are safe, as are their branches. Boil leaves first to make them sink and to disinfect them.

Aquatic plants

One of the added extras when keeping tropical fish, aquatic plants can bring both beauty and benefits to a freshwater aquarium.

When we look to nature, few bodies of freshwater come without some form of aquatic vegetation, be it growing in the shallow margins or wholly beneath the surface.

Aquatic plants provide oxygen and food for fish, a refuge for fish and fry, and can even purify tank water. Add plants to your aquarium and all of these benefits can be realised. It will look great too.

What plants need

Light

In order to survive underwater, aquatic plants need several things. Light is the first and most obvious requirement, as without light for an extended period all plants will die. Most of the plants kept in aquariums come from the tropical regions of the world, where the sun shines nearly every day, year round. To replicate this, you need to provide your plants with bright light for around ten hours every day.

Food

Next they need food. Land-based plants obtain their food through their roots alone, but aquatic plants obtain theirs through both their roots and their leaves.

Aquatic sands and gravels are generally inert and sterile, with no soil substitute to feed plants. A few very hardy species can just about get by on light and aquarium water alone, but the vast majority of aquatic plants need to be fed at the roots and through their leaves. To do this you must add a substrate fertiliser while setting up, before you place the gravel on top, and then add liquid fertilisers weekly or daily for the plants to take up through their leaves.

Carbon dioxide

Lastly, plants need carbon. This shouldn't be confused with the charcoal form of carbon that's used to chemically filter the water – plants take up their carbon from carbon dioxide.

In aquariums we generally discourage carbon dioxide in the water, as in high levels it can poison fish. But in a planted aquarium you actually need to add tiny amounts of CO_2 (though not enough to harm the fish), which the plants then use to help them grow. In return they produce oxygen, which aids the fish.

Plant choice

There are hundreds of plant species and cultivars available for aquariums. Coming either loose, in bunches or in pots, aquatic plants can be bought from aquatic stores or over the Internet.

They vary greatly in size, leaf shape, colour and difficulty, and a mixture of sizes, shapes and colours is generally used in forming an underwater garden. Many styles of 'gardening' can also be adopted, from formal styles where plants are placed in rows and arranged so that they heighten from front to back, to wild, jungle-looking styles that imitate a natural underwater scene, to natural arrangements in which the features of the rocks, wood, substrate and open water are just as important as the plants themselves. Whichever style you adopt, you must first master growing the plants themselves. Once you know how to cultivate aquatic plants successfully, you can concentrate on displaying them in such a way to enhance the look of your aquarium and the fish that swim between them.

Setting up

If you've opted to grow aquatic plants as well as to keep fish, your aquarium must be set up slightly differently. In order to provide the three things that plants need – light, food and carbon dioxide – lighting must be specially chosen, carbon dioxide injection equipment must be selected, and special planting substrates must be added, after the equipment goes in but before any other décor, the water or the plants.

Planting equipment

With plants and décor comes planting equipment. Just as in the garden, a variety of equipment and tools is available to help you achieve your goal.

Lighting

Lighting needs to be of the right colour spectrum and duration for aquatic plants if they're to grow. Full tropical sun is full spectrum, and when measured it has a colour temperature of 5,500K. Aquatic plants will grow under any bright lighting with a colour temperature between 2,000 and 10,000K, though lighting below 5,000K will look quite orange/yellow and won't enhance the colours of your fish. (See the lighting section on pages 26–9.)

Enhance fluorescent lighting with reflectors, and plug it into a timer for controlled lighting duration.

Yeast-based CO_2

Fuelled by the fermentation process, yeast-based systems use the by-product of fermentation, CO_2, to feed plants. Advantages of these systems are that they're inexpensive and safe to set-up, though the gas production can be slow to start, sporadic, and impossible to control. Yeast-based systems are more suited to beginners and small aquariums.

Pressurised CO_2

Regarded as the best way to introduce carbon dioxide, pressurised CO_2 systems comprise a pressurised CO_2 gas bottle, a pressure regulator to reduce gas pressure coming from the bottle and to finely control its release into the aquarium, and a diffuser. The regulator enables very fine adjustment by way of a needle valve, and optional extras like a solenoid, night shut-off valves and bubble counters can easily be fitted on. If you want a reliable supply of gas, then pressurised is the way to go, though due to the nature of the pressurised bottles they're unsuitable for young fishkeepers or complete novices. A regulator enables a variety of bottle sizes to be used.

Heating cable

Heating cables are used to produce a slow flow of oxygen and nutrients in soil-based substrates. The nutrients are slowly transported through the substrate by way of convection currents, and the whole substrate is turned into a slow biological filter.

CO₂ diffuser

This is essential for dissolving CO2 gas into water. Diffusers come in many forms, from plastic ladders and spirals to ceramic atomisers and venturi-style powerhead attachments. They all vary in price, design and effectiveness, though any style can be used. Ceramic diffusers often come with a glass

surround, and produce a fine mist of bubbles that relies on water circulation to distribute them and dissolve CO_2 into the water.

Ladder diffusers were popular in Europe at the end of the 20th century and work by achieving as much bubble/water contact time as possible and therefore maximum dissolving time. The bubble enters at the bottom of the diffuser and is forced through a series of baffles before it finally makes it to the surface. The longer it stays underwater, the more gas dissolves, and the smaller the bubble gets. Spiral diffusers work on the same principle.

Venturi diffusers work by injecting gas into the impeller chamber of a pump, which mashes up the bubbles into thousands of tiny ones, greatly increasing the surface area and the rate at which they dissolve into the water.

Drop checker

Also known as a permanent CO_2 indicator, a drop checker is placed inside the aquarium and indicates how much dissolved CO_2 is present by changing colour. By use of an indicator solution placed inside it, the blue liquid remains

blue if not enough CO_2 is present for the plants, green if the correct amount is present, and yellow if too much is present and at a level that's dangerous to fish. The colour changes can also be cross-referenced to measure both pH and the KH of the water.

Bubble counter

Suitable for pressurised or yeast-based CO_2 systems, a bubble counter is a glass or plastic device that provides a quick, at-a-glance check of how much CO_2 is entering the aquarium water. Bubble counters aren't necessary for some diffusers, as the

bubbles can be counted as they enter the diffuser at the bottom. Atomiser-type diffusers, however, will need one. They work very simply, producing countable bubbles of gas by passing it through a small quantity of water.

Planting tools

Tweezers

Tweezers can be very useful for planting individual delicate plants. For small species, planting with your fingers can be cumbersome, so tweezers are the better option, especially when you're planting into a dry substrate (*ie* before filling the tank), as fingers are likely to accidentally pull the tiny stem back out again as you try to let go. Although any tweezers can be used, aquatic tweezers are available that tend to be of a more convenient length. These come in a range of thicknesses.

Scissors

As with tweezers, any stainless steel scissors can be used, though aquatic-specific scissors are available with long

handles that make them look more like medical instruments. Scissors are used to cut roots when planting, or stems when pruning.

Planting

When you buy plants from a shop, or order them online, they will arrive in one of three different ways – as loose single plants, bunched, or potted. All three types will need to be prepared before planting.

Bunched plants

Bunched plants consist of several cuttings bundled together and then held at the bottom by a foam strip wrapped in a metal weight. The weight is there to hold the cuttings underwater and to keep them upright. The foam strip under the metal strip is to protect the delicate stems.

Although many species are available bunched, some do better than others when bought this way. As mentioned above, bunches typically contain cuttings of plants rather than a whole plant with roots at the bottom. Some species are fine when grown this way, including Cabomba, Myriophyllum and Hygrophila species, though plants with more complex root structures (and which use their roots more to gain nutrients), such as Amazon Swords and Cryptocorynes, are better bought potted.

To prepare a bunch for planting, remove the weight and foam strip at the bottom, revealing the loose cuttings. Plant each cutting separately 2–5cm apart, in order that some light can get through to the bottom and to discourage the stem from dropping its lower leaves and looking leggy and unsightly. To plant delicate stems use tweezers.

Potted plants

Regarded by many as the best way to purchase aquatic plants, these are entire growing plants complete with a full root system. The substrate in the pot consists of a material called mineral, a rock wool that the plants can anchor in and through which the nursery can feed liquid food to the roots. Although the plants will be growing fine in the mineral wool when you purchase them, you should remove as much of it as possible before planting in the aquarium substrate.

To do this, simply pull the pot off from the bottom and tease the wool away from the roots with your fingers. Once the wool is removed another key advantage of buying potted plants will be revealed – they often contain more than one growing specimen per pot. As with bunched plants, separate the individual stems and plant each one in the substrate 2–5cm from its nearest neighbour.

A root mass should be present on each plant, and to encourage new growth you should cut the root tips off before planting. Plant species with large root masses, such as

Amazon Sword plants, give you a clue that they need space in which to put out new roots and to grow, and demonstrate the importance that roots have in feeding the plant. Give lots of space to plants with large root masses, and plant them into nutritious substrates.

Single plants

This is the form in which plants often arrive when they're ordered online, or if you're given cuttings by a fellow plant-grower. They come nearly ready for

planting, though a quick trim of the roots should be carried out first. As with bunched and potted plants, you need to space them out and plant each stem separately. Delicate stems should be planted carefully using tweezers.

Snail removal

Unfortunately, some aquatic plants arrive carrying snails or their eggs. These pests are not wanted in a planted aquarium and need to be removed before you plant. Either pick them off by hand, rinse the plants under fast-running tap water or, best of all, bathe the plants in a snail-killing solution before planting.

Planting step by step – Bunched plants

1 Remove metal weight and foam strip from the base of the plants.

2 Separate out into individual plants.

3 Plant using tweezers, leaving ample space around each plant.

Planting step by step – Potted plants

1 Remove plastic pot.

2 Tease away the mineral wool from around the roots.

3 Separate out into individual plants.

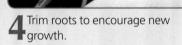

4 Trim roots to encourage new growth.

5 Plant leaving ample space around each plant.

Planting step by step – Single plants

1 Line up in readiness for planting.

2 Trim roots to encourage new growth.

3 Plant using tweezers, leaving ample space around each plant.

Plant species

Java Fern

Scientific name   Microsorum pteropus.
Size   Up to 30cm diameter and 30cm tall.
Origin   South-East Asia.
Lighting   Low to high.
Ease of keeping   Very easy.
Requirements   Rocks or wood upon which to anchor and grow.

Notes – Java Fern is one of the best aquatic plants available, as it is hardy, tough enough to be kept with large, boisterous fish, and provides an aged, natural look to any aquarium. It must not be planted in the substrate, but should instead be tied to rock or wood with fishing line or cotton thread, where it will eventually take root. It's a slow-growing species, with several cultivars available including Windelov and Narrow Fern. The species reproduces by developing small plantlets on the ends of its leaves.

Java Moss

Scientific name   Taxiphyllum barbieri (formerly Vesicularia dubyana).
Size   Fronds up to 5cm tall, but can spread across the whole aquarium.
Origin   South-East Asia.
Lighting   Low to high.
Ease of keeping   Easy.
Requirements   Rocks or wood upon which to anchor and grow.

Notes – Java Moss is a wonderful plant for any aquarium that looks great when growing on wood and rocks. It's hardy and may even be used by some fish for spawning. It spreads in all directions and can be propagated by division. Christmas Moss is a similar species, with an even more interesting frond formation. Use a good mechanical filter to keep the moss free of debris.

Crypts

Scientific name   Cryptocoryne sp.
Size   Up to 75cm, depending on species, but usually much shorter at around 15cm.
Origin   South-East Asia.
Lighting   Low to high.
Ease of keeping   Quite easy.
Requirements   A nutritious substrate and constant water conditions.

Notes – With their compact shape and dark green and red colours, Crypts are classic foreground plants. They're slow-growing and don't demand much light, though because of this they'll take some time to become established. Acclimatise them to your aquarium's temperature and water conditions, as they're grown out of the water in nurseries and new specimens can disintegrate in something known in the hobby as 'Crypt melt'. *Cryptocoryne balansae* is an exception to most short, foreground species, as it grows tall and should be placed at the rear of the aquarium. All Crypts spread by runners.

Amazon Sword plants

Scientific name	*Echinodorus sp.*
Size	Up to 75cm tall, though usually much smaller.
Origin	South America.
Lighting	Medium to bright.
Ease of keeping	Moderate.
Requirements	A nutritious substrate.

Notes – These are very popular aquarium plants, with *Echinodorus bleheri* being the most common. They're known as specimen plants and should be the centre of attention in the midground of your aquascape. Amazon Swords thicken out as they mature, and reproduce by sending out a rigid stem with new plants growing from it. These can be cut off and planted. Although collectively known as Amazon Swords, few if any originate from the River Amazon, which is largely devoid of plants.

Salvinia

Scientific name	*Salvinia natans.*
Size	5cm long by 2cm high.
Origin	Asia and Europe.
Lighting	Bright.
Ease of keeping	Quite easy.
Requirements	Still water at the surface, high humidity for optimum growth.

Notes – Salvinia is one of several floating plants available for the tropical aquarium. Traditionally it's used to block out excess light and soak up nutrients, starving algae, though it's also useful as a refuge for small fry, and as cover for surface-dwelling and bubble-nesting fish. It still needs to be fed with a liquid fertiliser, like any other aquarium plant, but it takes its CO_2 directly from the atmosphere. Too much Salvinia may block light to plants growing below it and hamper gaseous exchange at the surface.

Tropical water lilies

Scientific name	*Nymphaea sp.*
Size	Up to 90cm diameter and 90cm tall.
Origin	Found throughout the tropical regions of the world.
Lighting	Moderate to bright.
Ease of keeping	Moderate.
Requirements	Space, a nutritious substrate and slow-moving water.

Notes – Tropical water lilies are beautiful specimen plants that can be grown as a pond lily would be, with floating, waxy leaves and flowers; or those leaves can be pruned off regularly, forcing the plant to grow pretty underwater leaves. Coming as bulbs or tubers, lilies are hungry plants that need lots of food at the roots to spur fast leaf growth. Large aquariums are needed to show them at their best, or even tropical ponds. Too many surface leaves will block out light below, and lessen the surface area for gaseous exchange.

Green Cabomba

Scientific name   *Cabomba caroliniana.*
Size   Up to 90cm tall.
Origin   South America.
Lighting   Moderate to bright.
Ease of keeping   Easy.
Requirements   Very few.

Notes – Because of its fast growth and considerable height, Green Cabomba should be planted at the rear of an aquarium. It's easy to grow, requiring only light and liquid fertilisation, though strong light and CO_2 will generate phenomenal growth of many centimetres per week. Its feathery leaves make it a good space-filler, and egg-scattering fish may use it to spawn. It also provides refuge for small fry. It can be propagated by cutting off new plants, which grow from the stem, and doesn't need to root in the substrate. Red Cabomba is also available, though it's more demanding of light and CO_2.

Red Alternanthera

Scientific name   *Alternanthera reineckii.*
Size   50cm tall.
Origin   South America.
Lighting   Moderate to bright.
Ease of keeping   Moderate.
Requirements   Good lighting.

Notes – Red Alternanthera is often chosen to stand out amongst monotonous green plants, and is popular when planted in neat rows in Dutch-style aquariums. If given insufficient light and nutrients it may drop some of its lower leaves, and the remaining ones will turn green. Propagate by nipping out the top and replanting.

Glosso

Scientific name   *Glossostigma elatinoides.*
Size   5cm tall.
Origin   New Zealand.
Lighting   Bright.
Ease of keeping   Difficult.
Requirements   Bright light, high nutrient levels and
                                    high CO_2.

Notes – Unless you provide enough light, nutrients and CO_2 this species will be nearly impossible to grow underwater long-term, though if you provide it with everything it needs it will spread quickly across the substrate, creating a lawn effect that's very pleasing to the eye. Plant in individual plantlets initially, to prevent clumping, and then thin the lawn out regularly to prevent it from growing on top of itself.

Hygrophila Polysperma

Scientific name	*Hygrophila polysperma*.
Size	75cm tall.
Origin	South-East Asia.
Lighting	Moderate to bright.
Ease of keeping	Easy.
Requirements	Good lighting, a tall tank.

Notes – Polysperma is one of the easiest aquarium plants to grow and one of the fastest, increasing in height by many centimetres each week. It needs to be pruned regularly to keep it short, and pinching off the growing tip and replanting can achieve this. Cultivars with pink leaves are available, though some experts believe that pink hues can arise from a lack of fertilisation. Plant at the rear of the aquarium.

Anubias

Scientific name	*Anubias sp*.
Size	Up to 30cm tall.
Origin	West Africa.
Lighting	Low to bright.
Ease of keeping	Easy.
Requirements	Rocks or wood upon which it can anchor.

Notes – Anubias is a very hardy, slow-growing plant that's tolerant of low light and hard water and can be kept with tough, boisterous fish. It shouldn't be planted in the substrate but should instead be tied to wood or rocks using fishing line or cotton thread. Several species are available with leaves ranging in length from a few centimetres to about ten. Anubias brings a classic, old-world look to any aquarium.

Riccia

Scientific name	*Riccia fluitans*.
Size	1cm tall, spreads horizontally.
Origin	Worldwide.
Lighting	Bright.
Ease of keeping	Difficult.
Requirements	Bright light, high CO_2 levels.

Notes – Riccia can be grown in two ways – either as a floating plant (the way it lives in the wild), or as a submersed plant tied to wood or rocks. The first way is quite easy, as it will be close to the light at the surface and can obtain CO_2 from the atmosphere. The latter is much more difficult, as Riccia needs high levels of light and CO_2 in order to survive underwater, and it always floats back up to the surface after a short time. If you can get it to grow successfully underwater, the results can look stunning.

Vallis, Vallisneria

Scientific name	*Vallisneria sp.*
Size	Up to 180cm, but usually 90cm.
Origin	Worldwide.
Lighting	Medium to bright.
Ease of keeping	Moderately easy.
Requirements	A tall tank.

Notes – Vallis has the classic 'underwater grass' look, and is the type of plant that even non-fishkeepers will associate with streams and rivers. It's generally used in the background to provide height and a natural look to a planting scheme, and also to hide equipment such as filters and heaters. It grows too tall for most tanks, spreading horizontally across the surface, but even this can be a desirable feature and again adds to the natural look. Vallis spreads by runner from the roots and can be a prolific grower, though it prefers hard water with calcium. Prune simply by removing runners or cutting the leaves in half, forcing new growth.

Rotala

Scientific name	*Rotala sp.*
Size	Around 60cm tall.
Origin	South-East Asia.
Lighting	Bright.
Ease of keeping	Moderate to difficult.
Requirements	Bright light, CO_2.

Notes – Plant experts prize Rotala, as they're difficult to grow but look stunning if you succeed with them. There are several species, two red ones and several green ones, and the leaves vary from quite large spade-shaped ones on the red *Rotala rotundifolia*, to fine, needle-shaped leaves on the other red Rotala and the variety known simply as *Rotala sp.* '*Green*'. Rotala must have brighter-than-average lighting and high levels of CO_2 if it's to do well, and although commonly available only experienced plant growers succeed with it. Once growing well it requires regular pruning by cutting off the growing tips.

Bolbitis

Scientific name	*Bolbitis heudelotii.*
Size	About 30cm tall and 30cm wide.
Origin	West Africa.
Lighting	Low to bright.
Ease of keeping	Moderate to difficult.
Requirements	Rocks or wood upon which to grow.

Notes – Bolbitis is a popular fern for West African biotope aquariums. It's slow-growing and needs good lighting, strong flow and high nutrients in order to do well. It has an interesting leaf structure that when used in bogwood provides a mature, aged look. It's hardy enough to be combined with boisterous fish, as its leaves aren't craved by those that like to nibble plants. However, because of its slow growth it's hard to tell how well the plant is actually doing. Combine it with mosses for a classic look.

Pogostemon

Scientific name	*Pogostemon helferi*.
Size	5cm tall.
Origin	Thailand.
Lighting	Moderate to bright.
Ease of keeping	Moderate.
Requirements	Light and CO_2.

Notes – Pogostemon is a relative newcomer to the hobby, though it's already proving very popular. It has a unique star shape when viewed from above and tough, crinkled leaves. Its short height means that it should be planted in the foreground. If it's provided with enough light, CO_2 and nutrients it spreads by runner, producing a carpet of new plants that are eye-catching and fill the foreground nicely.

Hemianthus Cuba, HC

Scientific name	*Hemianthus callitrichoides cuba*.
Size	3cm tall.
Origin	Cuba.
Lighting	Very bright.
Ease of keeping	Difficult.
Requirements	Bright light, CO_2, nutrients.

Notes – Hemianthus Cuba is another relative newcomer that has proved very popular as a foreground plant, though it's not easy to grow and generally only expert growers succeed with it. It's one of the smallest plants available, and spreads by runner, making a tight, compact carpet of green in the foreground of aquariums with very bright lighting. Its compact shape looks very neat, and it's already a favoured species amongst serious aquascapers who turn their aquariums into works of art. Buy it fresh from the grower, as it will quickly deteriorate in conditions that are anything less than optimum.

Hairgrass

Scientific name	*Eleocharis sp*.
Size	Up to 30cm tall.
Origin	Worldwide.
Lighting	Bright.
Ease of keeping	Moderate to difficult.
Requirements	Bright light, CO_2.

Notes – Hairgrass grows above the waterline in nature, so needs bright light and CO_2 if it's to do well when grown underwater. As its name suggests, it's incredibly slender, and splitting it into individual plantlets may seem impossible, yet it can be done. Two species are regularly available – *Eleocharis acicularis* and the dwarf *Eleocharis parvula*. In tiny tanks, *E. acicularis* can be used as a background plant, but *E. parvula* is almost always used in the foreground. As Hairgrass grows, it forms dense mats that can cover the whole substrate. It can be pruned easily by cutting it short with scissors, and it propagates by sending out runners. In tanks with insufficient light it won't survive, and it will decompose within just a few days of being transported, so make sure that your source is fresh – ideally another hobbyist who's already growing it successfully underwater.

Aquascaping

'Aquascaping' is the term applied to decorating an aquarium. Every aquarium has had a certain amount of aquascaping done on it, as the décor has been arranged and put into place.

It has a dual purpose – to make the tank visually appealing, and to provide a suitable home for your fish. Proper aquascaping will, in fact, make the difference between an OK-looking aquarium and a great one. If you're aquascaping for the breeding requirements of a specific fish, for example a cave-dwelling cichlid, it can even be the difference between them breeding or not breeding.

Most aquascaping is done while the aquarium is being set up, although some aquascapes – such as planted tanks or marine reef aquariums – will continue to subtly change over time as the organisms grow and spread within them.

Before any aquascaping is done, the correct type of décor must be chosen (see pages 36–7). This must be specific to the type of set-up that you're creating, such as a nutritious substrate for planted tanks, calcareous rock and substrate for marine tanks, and inert rocks and substrate for

Left: Ornamental designs are enchanting and popular with new fishkeepers.

freshwater tanks. Get the aquascaping materials wrong and your aquarium may not run as it should.

Look at the textures of the décor too, and its functionality, as goldfish could get stuck in small caves or holes, and algae-grazing fish won't appreciate the rough surface of Lava rock.

But apart from the functional side of aquascaping, it's basically about creating a little piece of art. Borrow design features from elsewhere to create an aquatic masterpiece. Choose décor that complements the colours of your fish, and design features that catch the eye, and arrange your plants or rock in groups to enhance their visual appeal.

The ornamental look

Ornamental designs are popular with new fishkeepers, or those who like to see order in their lives and in their aquariums. An ornamental design will look man-made, and will contain such things as sunken ships, replica rocks or wood and arranged plants and corals, either real or replica.

Ornamental tanks can look very neat, and as long as they function the fish won't be bothered either way. Bright, unnatural colours can be used for both substrate and décor,

Below: The natural look is challenging but popular with more seasoned fishkeepers.

The biotope

The biotope aquarium takes the natural-looking tank one step further, as it replicates an actual location from nature, be it an African lake, an Amazonian stream or an area of coral reef.

In the biotope, fish are only added if they're from the selected location, and décor is chosen and aquascaped so that it looks just like the actual environment. If the décor, water conditions and species are all matched to a specific biotope, the fish should be very happy, as you'll have created a 'home from home'. They should behave more naturally, show better colour, and may even breed.

Finding specific plant or coral species is usually more difficult than choosing the fish, as more data is generally available on the latter than on their environment. However, as long as you get it as close as you can that's all that matters.

Leave them out!

One aspect of the natural world that *shouldn't* feature in a biotope aquarium is that of predators and prey. In the wild the prey fish have a chance to escape in the vast body that is their home, but in the confines of an aquarium they have nowhere to go, which makes them very stressed and puts them on the menu to be eaten. So only select biotope-correct fish that will live together in harmony.

Below: A biotope aquarium is designed to mimic an exact habitat, and its fish.

though in such cases the fish will prefer darker colours, as these make them feel more relaxed.

Ornamental designs can take on any theme or look, as they only have to satisfy the aquascaper's personal tastes. Themes could include an underwater Atlantis, an arranged flowerbed or a planted tank in which everything is neatly aligned.

The natural look

More popular with seasoned fishkeepers, these take inspiration from nature and attempt to replicate it in the aquarium, making our fish feel more at home and presenting onlookers with a fascinating view of the underwater world.

Using natural materials to create such tanks has many advantages for fish, as it encourages them to behave just as they would in the wild, swimming amongst plants, hiding under stones and sunken wood, camouflaging themselves, grazing algae and even breeding.

Cycling

Before you add fish to any aquarium it must be matured and made ready to break down their waste. This process is called cycling.

Why cycle?

Fish produce waste as they breathe, and defecate. In the wild this waste is washed away and diluted by the sheer magnitude of the volume of water in which they live, and they aren't adapted to live in their own waste products.

In the confines of an aquarium, this presents the fishkeeper with a challenge, as the fish are constantly polluting the water that they're in but at the same time can't tolerate living in polluted water.

A filter will help to deal with the mechanical, solid waste that fish produce, and will help to clear the water, but the invisible presence that really breaks down harmful fish waste is bacteria.

Cycling is the process of introducing bacteria, providing them with a home and establishing a viable population.

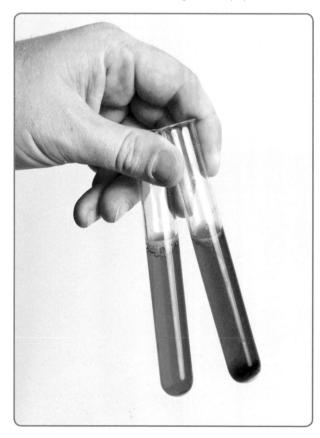

Keeping your bacteria healthy

A wise fishkeeper will often tell you that to keep good fish, you first need to keep good water. To maintain a healthy population of beneficial bacteria, provide them with a good home in the form of filter media and oxygen, either from a good flow of water through the filter or from bubbles from an airstone. Bacteria need to breathe too.

How to cycle

As soon as the aquarium has been filled with water, the filter has been plugged in and the water has been dechlorinated, it will be ready for bacteria. Chlorine and chloramines kill bacteria, so must be removed first.

Next you need to introduce bacteria of the correct type and quantity. The easiest way to do this is buy an off-the-shelf bacterial starter mix and simply pour the bacteria into the water as directed.

Fishless cycling

Without fish waste, the bacteria will not have anything to feed on and will diminish in numbers and die off. The simple answer would be to introduce some fish, only the level of pollutants present might not be effectively removed by a new bacteria colony and the water parameters may shift, causing severe stress to the fish or even killing them.

The safest way both to introduce bacteria and to prepare the colony for fish is to 'fishless cycle'. Fishless cycling involves adding bacteria (again by means of an off-the-shelf treatment) and also a synthetic ammonia source to feed the bacteria by simulating the presence of fish.

Ammonia can be bought in its raw form from a chemist, or in a more fishkeeper-friendly form from an aquatic store.

Fishless cycling is the most ethical way to mature aquariums, as the fish aren't exposed to any pollutants. Using hardy fish to cycle a tank is no longer considered acceptable.

TIP

When fishless cycling, you need to test the water every day, and keep a record of the ammonia levels, the subsequent nitrite levels, and finally nitrates. Only when all the ammonia has disappeared along with all the nitrite is the aquarium cycled and ready for fish. This may take several weeks.

Other ways to cycle

Bacteria can be introduced from mature aquariums that have an established fish population. Run two filters in an existing tank, and move one over to the new tank, making it instantly ready for fish. Failing that, transferring some water and/or some of the substrate from an existing tank can also introduce vital bacteria.

'Live' substrates are also available that come packed in water, complete with bacteria and food to keep them alive while in transport. These can be used to boost the bacteria levels in an existing set-up or to give a newly set up aquarium a biological kick-start.

Just add fish!

Some bacterial starters are advanced enough to claim that they can instantly make an aquarium ready for a population of fish. Indeed, the nature of the bacterial strains used means that they actually need the ammonia produced by fish in order to stay alive.

It is the author's opinion, however, that such products should be used with caution, and that a little patience, and cycling more slowly, is better in the long run. But such starters do have some practical advantages, being great for replenishing bacterial populations after medications have been used or mature media have been accidentally over-washed, and also when changing mature media for new.

New tank syndrome

If a tank is set up, and fish introduced too quickly, an all too common problem occurs. The fish start to produce waste, but there is insufficient bacteria to break down that waste, and pollutants build up to dangerous levels, making the fish ill and even killing them. A new tank with water quality problems, and too many fish, too soon, is suffering from New Tank Syndrome.

TIP

Never add maturation fluids to untreated tap water. The chlorine in tap water will kill both good and bad bacteria.

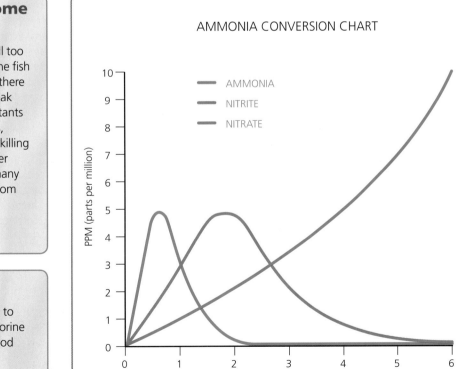

Setting up a tank

Now that you have an idea about what's required to run an aquarium, it's time to set one up. This is one of the best parts of fishkeeping, as you get to realise your dream and bring life and colour to your living room.

Getting started

Preparation is key when setting up an aquarium, as it's important that you get it right first time. Make sure that you have everything you need in terms of equipment, décor and water conditioners, and clear a space around where the aquarium will be set up so that you have room to move and can lay out equipment and décor in readiness to go into the aquarium.

Remember that you'll need close proximity to electrical points, and typically will need a multi-socket that can take plugs for three or more appliances – the filter, heater and light. More complex tanks, such as marine aquariums, may need many more electrical sockets, and this should all be sorted out before you start to fill the aquarium with water.

Decide how you're going to fill the aquarium. If you're using tap water you'll either need a hosepipe or a clean bucket to transfer it from the sink to the tank. A hose is easier on your back, but it can make a mess if it's forgotten about or if it falls out of the aquarium while it's left unattended during filling.

Maybe you won't be using tap water at all and have opted instead for the greater purity of reverse osmosis (RO) water. If you have, then you'll either need to buy enough from an aquatic shop to fill the aquarium, or to make up

your own days in advance using your own unit. ROs run much more slowly than the average tap does.

Décor

Décor will need to be rinsed before being placed in the aquarium, especially the gravel. Rocks and wood should also be rinsed off. As mentioned earlier, it's worth checking that the wood will automatically sink when you buy it, as not all wood does. If it doesn't, pre-soak it in readiness. It's a good idea to pre-soak all wood anyway if you don't want it to leach tannins and stain the water brown.

Substrates must be washed in order to remove dust, as they've been quarried and will be full of dirt that will cloud the aquarium water. Place them in a bucket, colander or sieve and rinse vigorously with tap water until the water runs clear. Several more buckets will be needed to hold the clean gravel until it's placed in the aquarium.

People power

Nothing is ever straightforward when setting up an aquarium, so give yourself plenty of time. Work out how long you think it is going to take you and then double it, as these things shouldn't be rushed. Equipment must be fitted properly and decor should be placed the way you want it right from the start. Once the aquarium is filled with water moving things around is far less easy, and will normally result in particles being stirred up and clouding the water.

Left: Buckets are essential when keeping fish.

BELOW: Keep the area around your aquarium dry with a towel.

Above: Décor must be rinsed before use, to remove dust.

Above: Preparation is essential before setting up a tank.

Setting up a medium to large-sized aquarium is a physical job, so get someone to help you, preferably with previous experience. At the very least they can wash the gravel and rinse the décor. More to the point, have you thought about how you're going to move the empty tank and cabinet into position without help, or, if it still needs unwrapping, who's going to lift it while the packaging is removed? An extra body can also turn the hose on and off for you in another room, or hold external filter pipes in position while you cut them to fit. If you've forgotten something fundamental they could even dash to the aquatic store to get it for you. All this will save valuable time and minimise stress.

Be prepared

Buy more dechlorinator than you need, just in case you miscalculated the tank volume or have to remove the water and start again. Put plenty of towels on the floor to catch drips, as there will be lots of these, and wear old clothes, as you're bound to get wet. Lastly, set the tank up on a day and at a time that your local aquatic store will be open. Otherwise you'll be caught out if your filter doesn't switch on when it should, or you need extra supplies and can't get them.

Reverse Osmosis and its uses

Commonly abbreviated to RO, Reverse Osmosis is a water purification process. Its origins lie in industry and science, where a very pure grade of water is necessary, and the quality of mains tap water is not good enough to achieve that.

An RO unit connects to a mains water pipe and purifies tap water by forcing it at pressure through a very fine membrane, resulting in water that may be 99% pure. Before being forced through the membrane, the water is prefiltered through a sediment filter to remove solids, and then through a carbon filter to remove chlorine, as both will negatively affect the ability of the RO membrane to purify the water. As well as pure (product) water, an RO unit will also produce waste water, that contains all the minerals and organic contaminants removed by the membrane.

Why is RO water useful for fish?

As good as tap water is for humans, there are many additives like chlorine for example that make it bad for fish and bad for friendly filter bacteria that we are trying to encourage. RO is free of chlorine, minerals that raise pH and GH, and organic pollutants like phosphates and nitrates, which can cause nuisance algae growth. By using this pure water in our aquariums we then don't need to dechlorinate it, it is less likely to cause algae growth than by using normal tap water, and because it is free of minerals, it is very soft which is perfect for fish that like soft water, with a low pH, like Discus. It is also very useful for marines, as when mixed with marine salt it won't contain or add any phosphate, nitrate or chlorine, which are all harmful to marine organisms.

A Deioniser or DI, purifies tap water but to an even higher grade than RO, and doesn't produce waste water, though is a more expensive method. An RO/DI in combination can get the best results and water purification standards.

Coldwater step-by-step

Coldwater fish, and goldfish in particular, are often the first fish that anyone keeps. Set up a proper tank for them in the first place and they'll offer you years of enjoyment and relaxation.

What goldfish really need is space, good food, good water quality from a filter, a regular maintenance regime, and suitable tank-mates. *Never* try to keep them in unfiltered bowls.

The tank pictured in this section will provide a suitable long-term home for fancy goldfish and is easy to set up and maintain. Since plastic plants are used the light only needs to be on for viewing the fish, and with no heater it's also a low-energy set-up.

Goldfish are the perfect choice for those who want big blocks of colour, and not too much of their time to be taken up. Fancy goldfish have cute faces that appeal to children, and a peaceful disposition.

1 Choose a suitably sized aquarium for coldwater fish. Remember that goldfish grow large, are messy feeders and require more space and oxygen than tropical fish. Any aquarium less than 90cm in length should be considered only short-term accommodation for single-tailed varieties.

2 Fit the filter, which in this case is an internal power filter. This will cope with the solid waste from the goldfish, has an adjustable flow and is relatively inexpensive, though an external filter is a better choice as it can handle more waste. An internal filter should be fitted inside the top rear corner of the aquarium so that its outlet nozzle is just below the surface. Don't switch the filter on until the aquarium is filled with water.

3 Thoroughly rinse some 3–5mm diameter pea gravel, and place to a depth of 5cm all across the aquarium base. Pea gravel has been chosen as it's easy to keep clean with a gravel vacuum, and the particle size and smooth edges make it easy for the goldfish to mouth as they search through it for food.

4 Place the large decoration next, such as rocks or wood. For fancy goldfish the decor must be smooth so that they don't catch themselves on any sharp edges; and don't use any caves or hollow decor that they could get stuck inside, as they aren't good at reversing. Smooth pebbles have been chosen for this set-up.

5 Plastic plants provide extra decorative elements in this case, as goldfish eat live plants. Arrange tall ones at the back, medium-sized ones in the middle, and short ones at the front. Place gravel around the bases of the plants to anchor them down.

6 Fill with water using a hose or a bucket. To prevent shifting the gravel or décor as you do this, use a colander to deflect the flow. Fill to within a few centimetres of the top, or to the fill-line that comes inside some aquariums. Cold tap water will be fine for goldfish, and will warm up steadily over the next few days until it reaches room temperature.

7 Dechlorinate. As this is a newly set up aquarium being filled for the first time, it can be filled first and then dechlorinated afterwards, but for all future water-changes the water must be dechlorinated first before it comes into contact with either the fish or the filter bacteria. Use dechlorinator as directed for new aquariums.

8 Plug in the filter. This will start to move the water around the aquarium and will help to distribute the dechlorinator. Leave for five or ten minutes for the dechlorinator to work properly and make the water safe.

9 Add filter bacteria. This will bring the first bit of biological life to your new aquarium, though it will still not be ready for fish.

10 Connect up the light, fit it into the hood and plug it into a light timer. Place the hood on the tank. Check that the filter is running as it should be, and that it's at the right height so that it agitates the surface water and introduces oxygen. Venturi devices are good for goldfish, as are air pumps.

11 Begin fishless cycling by adding an ammonia source and testing daily with a test kit until ammonia and nitrite have both peaked, and then gone down to zero. Then add the first fish.

12 The finished tank. Six fancy goldfish will be fine for this sort of set up, and it is very easy to maintain, with a simple layout.

Tropical step-by-step

Tropical fish come in so many varieties that they're suitable for fishkeepers of all abilities, budgets and skill levels. The aquarium set-up below is suitable for beginners and is straightforward to create and maintain. An internal filter has been used in this example, but an external power filter could be used instead. Hardy live plants have been chosen to create a natural look, though plastic plants could be used as an alternative.

If you're new to tropical fish, choose hardy species that are easy to keep and won't grow too large. Tropical aquariums can hold more fish per volume than coldwater or marine ones, enabling a busy look to be achieved with lots going on and all sorts of different body shapes and colours.

Using this step-by-step guide as a template, the aquarium could easily be adapted to become a biotope aquarium, a breeding aquarium or one for specimen or oddball fish.

1 The size of a tropical aquarium must be matched to its inhabitants. For a community of several groups of small to medium-sized fish, an aquarium of 80–100cm is necessary. Don't add any fish species that attain an average body length of more than 10cm, as all fish will need room to swim.

2 Fit the filter, or in this case the filter already comes built in. This systemised aquarium comes with a factory fitted internal filter containing three types of filter media to filter mechanically, biologically and chemically. If opting for an external filter, place the filter body in the cabinet underneath and connect up the pipe work.

3 Tropical fish require a heater/ thermostat. Place this on the rear glass, at an angle, where it will receive water flow, or in this case fit it inside the filter. Set it to the required temperature, but don't plug in either the heater or the filter until the aquarium is filled with water. If setting up a tank for large tropical fish, or catfish, a heater guard should be fitted to protect them from being burnt by the hot element, and to protect the heater from being damaged by the fish.

4 Wash the substrate and place it over the bottom of the aquarium to a depth of 5cm. Plants will be used, but aren't the main focus of this tropical set-up, so any colour and grain size can be used. If you're intending to add bottom-scavenging catfish like Corydoras to the set-up, fine sands are best, enabling them to sift the substrate as they look for food.

5 Add the large décor next, which in this case consists of three large rocks, and a smaller rock. The rocks are placed off centre in a key focal point, with three stacked together and the smaller one opposite. When decorated with plants it will offer a natural look.

6 Fill the aquarium with water. If you wish to keep soft water fish in an Amazonian biotope, for example, reverse osmosis water is the best choice. Cold water can be added at this stage, as no tropical fish will be added for several weeks.

7 Dechlorinate to make the water safe for fish and filter bacteria. Use as directed for new aquariums. If using pure RO water, add minerals and electrolytes (see page xxx) which are essential for all fish. Plug in the filter to help circulate the dechlorinator, and the heater can be plugged in and switched on at this stage too. Both should run continuously.

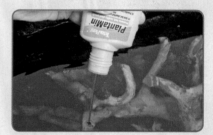

8 Add filter bacteria in readiness for cycling.

9 Place some hardy live plants amongst the décor, placing the tallest species at the back. Tall, feathery Cabomba has been used as a space filler as it will also help to hide the filter box from view. Continue planting placing specimen plants in the midground and small, carpeting plants at the front.

10 Add some liquid plant food to help the live plants establish. For a more in-depth planted set-up see pages 60–1.

11 Fit the light into the hood, and plug into a light timer. Plant growth/fish colour-enhancing light tubes are recommended. Fit a thermometer for temperature monitoring, add an ammonia source and begin fishless cycling. Only add fish when nitrite and ammonia levels are back down to zero.

12 The finished tank. The vast choice of tropical fish allows colour, movement and activity to be achieved at all levels, by choosing fish that live at the surface, in the middle and at the bottom. Use algae-eating fish to keep nuisance algae to a minimum.

Planted step-by-step

The planted aquarium goes a step further than the normal tropical aquarium, as a key part of its attraction is its healthy plants and the way that they're laid out.

From the very material out of which the tank has been manufactured, every detail has been researched and thought out so that not only are the plants and fish provided with the best possible conditions, but the tank looks as good as it can too.

The aquarium in the example depicted is made from clearer than normal glass called Opti-White, which is low in iron and looks clear even when you look through its edges. To create a minimalist look the tank doesn't even have a rim or bracing bars on the top, and the lighting comes from a

'luminaire' that sits over the tank on legs instead of being fitted in a standard hood.

The idea with this style of planted aquarium is to create a miniature work of art that's alive with fish and plants. This type of set-up is referred to by some as high-tech, since although small it comes with very bright lighting and a large external filter and is fertilised on a daily basis. With these ingredients any type of aquatic plant can be grown, and due to the bright lighting even difficult plants can be grown right at the bottom, where they will grow tight and low, providing an effect similar to a lawn in a garden. This style of aquarium, decor and planting is very popular in the Far East, where hobbyists take their inspiration from nature.

Here's how to make a stunning planted aquarium.

1 Tank and cabinet. The clean-cut look is designed to ensure minimal distraction from the aquascape when complete. The hole in the side is for filter hoses.

2 Add a layer of substrate fertiliser. This is essential for growing healthy plants, as it will provide them with food at the roots.

3 Cover the substrate fertiliser with fine gravel or coarse sand. This will provide the plants with anchorage and will prevent the fine fertiliser from being disturbed and getting into the water column. Black has been chosen to complement the fish and plant colours.

4 Next add the 'hardscape', the wood and some of the rocks. These will become key focal points, so take your time when placing them and don't be afraid to have several goes at it before any water is added.

5 This tank will have the foreground entirely covered with plants. This job is done first as it takes the most time. (Note that in standard aquariums the background plants are added first.)

6 More plants are added, this time around the back and sides. You can begin to see the planting scheme coming together now. Spray with water to keep the plants moist until the aquarium is set up.

7 Java fern is placed between the wood and the rocks and will itself become a key aquascaping feature. The red plant behind it will grow tall and will also attract the eye.

8 CO_2 and external filter equipment is added next. Note the clear glass design of both the CO_2 equipment and the filter pipe work. Known as 'glassware', clear glass equipment is popular in planted tanks, again because it doesn't detract from the plants themselves.

9 Fill with dechlorinated water. Make sure that it's at least at room temperature before filling so as not to shock the plants, and fill very slowly and gradually so that the substrate and the delicate planting at the front aren't disturbed.

10 This picture inside the cabinet shows the external filter, connected to an inline heater to remove it from the tank, and the gas bottle for the pressurised CO_2 system. Liquid fertilisers can be stored in there too.

11 Add the fertilisers and plug in the heater and filter. Set the lights to come on for ten hours per day, and begin to mature the filter with maturation agents and a test kit. Only add the first fish when the tank has been fishless cycled.

12 The finished tank. The plants are showing visible growth after just a few weeks and the clean, crisp design will grace any living room or office.

Lake Malawi step-by-step

This Malawi set-up demonstrates just how varied tropical freshwater aquariums can be. Décor can be made up of coral sand and calcareous rocks like ocean rock for a marine look and something that is quite different from the norm, though natural looking boulders and sand have been chosen here instead.

Malawi cichlids – from Lake Malawi in East Africa's Rift Valley, where they're called Mbuna – are great if you're looking for colour and movement. Their stunning display of bright blues and yellows causes some people to mistake them for marine fish, and they can certainly provide the look of marines without all the added care, equipment and expense.

Naturally inhabiting rocky shores in well-oxygenated alkaline water, Malawi cichlids must have rocky aquariums in which to feed and to breed. In the wild they graze algae along the shoreline and fight to hold the best territories. To overcome their territorial nature in the aquarium, we overcrowd them, so that one fish has less chance of ruling the whole tank and picking on others. Malawi cichlids will readily breed in an aquarium set-up like this, with the females holding the eggs and fry in their mouths before spitting the larger fry amongst the rocks to fend for themselves.

1 Choose a large tank for keeping Malawi cichlids, as you'll be adding a lot of them. They average 15cm in length and are active, aggressive fish. In this instance a 120cm-long aquarium has been selected.

2 Fit the filter, which in this case is a large, powerful external filter capable of dealing with all the waste that this overcrowded tank will create. Place the filter body in the cabinet underneath, layer the media as directed, and check that the sealing ring and impeller cover are in place. Fit the rigid inlet and outlet pipes inside the aquarium, and connect up with the flexible hosepipes. Cut the hose to length for a neat job.

3 Malawi cichlids are tropical fish, so will require a heater thermostat. Choose a model large enough for the volume of water and fit a heater guard, as rockwork will be placed near to the delicate heater. Stick it on the back glass, where it will receive flow from the filter, aiding temperature distribution.

4 Because this tank will be overcrowded, additional aeration has been chosen in the form of an airstone, driven by an air pump. Connect the pump outside the aquarium to a non-return valve, airline and finally the airstone. Use clips and suckers to hold the airstone in place.

5 Add the rocks, and build them up into a pile that spans the back of the aquarium and provides lots of caves and hideouts for the fish. Any rock can be used in Malawi cichlid aquariums and calcareous varieties can be chosen to help buffer the pH and hardness of the water, and also to create a pseudo-marine look. Place the rocks straight onto the bottom of the tank, so that that fish can't dig beneath them and cause a rock fall. Stack the largest, flattest first, fitting them into place as you go. Lean the whole pile against the back glass for added stability. Give the rocks an occasional shake as you proceed, to check that they won't fall over.

6 Rinse and then place the substrate around the base of the rocks. No other décor has been used, so as not to distract from the fish, which are the main attraction.

7 Fill the tank with tap water. Expect some cloudiness for the first few days, but the filter will soon make it crystal clear.

8 Dechlorinate, adding enough to treat the total volume of water in the tank.

9 Prime the filter, turn it on and turn the air pump on. Between them these will circulate the water and thereby aid the dechlorination process. Plug in and turn on the heater.

10 Add filter bacteria in readiness for fishless cycling. The vigorously aerated water will aid the reproduction of nitrifying bacteria.

11 Add an ammonia source, test the water daily and don't add any fish until ammonia and nitrite have peaked and returned to zero. Use a thermometer to monitor temperature.

12 The finished tank, with a very different look to the standard tropical fish aquarium. The stark sand and rock will contrast with the bright fish colours and the whole scene will look clean and modern. Since Malawi cichlids must be overstocked in order to keep aggression to a minimum, a 120cm Malawi cichlid aquarium must contain 20 or more similarly sized fish.

Paludarium

A paludarium is part aquarium, part planted tank, part ornament, and again demonstrates just how varied the tropical fish hobby can be. The name 'paludarium' comes from the Latin word *palus*, meaning 'marsh', and is basically a planted aquarium that's half-filled with decor and plants growing through the surface.

You may wonder why you'd actually want half as much water as normal, giving way to terrestrial plants and areas of dry land. The answer is that a paludarium can provide the perfect habitat for semi-aquatic creatures such as crabs, frogs and newts, while the water section can become home to tiny marshland fish such as Killies and Bettas.

What's more, many aquatic plants are actually semi-aquatic, having their roots in water but their foliage out in the open air. This way they can take advantage of the abundant light and CO_2 while also having access to a permanent water supply and source of nutrients.

A paludarium can be made from anything that will hold water, though an aquarium or glass terrarium is best. Use aquarium lighting to enhance plant growth, bogwood and rocks to create the land area, and combine aquatic and terrestrial plants to create a fabulous miniature world. Clever use of an internal filter can create a waterfall, adding to the visual effect of the paludarium while also providing extra humidity at the upper level for the terrestrial plants and an area for moisture-loving species such as mosses and ferns.

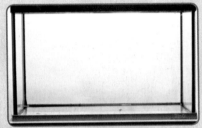

1 Choose a suitable aquarium. This one is 60cm long and quite tall, providing a good-sized viewing area above the water, and sufficient depth in which to keep fish below.

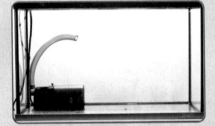

2 Install an internal filter. The difference with fitting this model is that it will be placed on its back underwater in the rear corner so that it can run in the shallow water, but will also be connected to a piece of PVC hose that will be used to power a waterfall.

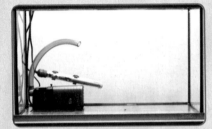

3 Install the heater. Again it will need to be placed flat to make sure that it's always under the water. Set it to normal tropical temperatures, and if using it near rocks fit a heater guard.

4 Start to build a stack of rocks and wood. In the corner with the internal filter build a stack of rocks that will become the waterfall. To do this place large rocks at the bottom, small ones on top, and tier them so that they slope front to back. Place the PVC filter pipe in the top rear corner of the rock stack.

5 Place gravel on the bottom. Any gravel will do but this red baked clay is good for plant growth, and matches the red of the lava rock waterfall. Place to a depth of 5cm, and if you want substantial underwater plant growth put a substrate fertiliser down too.

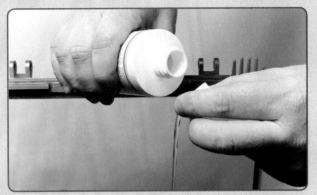

6 Part-fill the tank with water to provide a water depth of around 10–15cm. This will leave enough space above the waterline for planting, but crucially will cover the filter and heater, and leave enough depth for some tiny tropical fish.

7 Dechlorinate to make the water safe for fish, plants and amphibians. Tap water will be fine in most cases, unless you're going to keep fish that require very soft water.

8 Turn on the waterfall, and move the rocks if necessary to create the desired effect. The waterfall should splash down the rocks and recirculate, providing an excellent area for moisture-loving amphibians and plants. To get the waterfall just right choose an internal filter or pump with adjustable flow. Ensure the waterfall flow is the way you want it before adding any further decoration.

9 Add filter bacteria to seed the tank in readiness for cycling. Add an ammonia source next, and test the water daily until ammonia and nitrite have peaked and then returned to zero.

10 Introduce small aquatic plants and floating plants to start off the marsh effect.

11 Place large terrestrial plants amongst the rocks and wood at the top to create overhanging vegetation.

12 The finished tank. Paludariums can be any size, from very small to very large and elaborate, and because of their dual habitats they're suitable for a huge number of fish, plants and amphibians. The waterfall and terrestrial plants add to the beauty of a paludarium.

COLDWATER & TROPICAL FISH

Buying fish

Buying fish is one the most fun parts of the hobby, and after all that attention to detail while setting up, it's what you've been waiting for!

It's important, however, not to make any rash decisions. The decisions that you make in the aquatic shop will affect your whole aquarium in the long-term, and if you make the wrong ones it could cause you no end of stress, which is not what fishkeeping is about.

Make a list

It helps if you have an idea of what you want before you go into the shop. Once there you'll be overwhelmed by the sheer variety of choices available, and you if you're not careful you'll stray from what you should be buying and take a risk on something that's not suitable.

Peruse the fish profile pages at the rear of this book and make a list of the species that you like, and those that are suitable to be mixed with each other. From that list, determine which are the most hardy, and thus the most suitable to be your first fish. Even the largest, most mature aquariums won't be ready to take more than about ten fish in one go, while a good number for medium-sized tropicals is about six. Six is considered a small shoal, and shoaling species like Neon tetras would be happy in groups of six or more.

Once in the shop, stick to your list, as you know that the fish you've chosen will mix with each other and won't outgrow your tank. If your retailer doesn't have any of the fish you really want, nor even any of your second or third choices, resist the enormous temptation to buy another type that's not on your list. Either try elsewhere or ask your retailer to order them in for you.

Make sure that they're healthy

This isn't an easy task for the untrained eye, but if the shop does stock the fish that you want, take a good look at them to make sure they look healthy. A healthy fish should have clear eyes, intact fins and be active (unless it's a sedate catfish). It shouldn't have any stringy faeces attached, and although its gills should be moving as it breathes the movements shouldn't be too erratic or laboured.

Signs of an unhealthy fish are white spots, white patches and fungus, indicating disease. These should be left alone. Also avoid any fish that are gasping, hanging just below the surface (unless they're meant to be there, such as hatchetfish), swimming erratically, or refusing food when offered it.

Check that they're feeding

A healthy fish will always be on the lookout for food, and you can make use of this characteristic when you're buying. If you're unsure about the health of a particular fish, ask the retailer to offer it a small amount of food. It should then become active and eat it. If it doesn't, it's either unhealthy due to disease, unhealthy due to poor water quality in its tank, or has been newly imported, perhaps from the wild, and is not ready to feed due to transportation stress or unfamiliarity with prepared foods. Whatever the reason, a fish that isn't feeding isn't ready to go home with you.

Ask lots of questions

A good retailer should be asking you questions about the suitability of your tank, and you should in turn be asking them questions about the suitability of the species for your tank. If a shop lets you just have the fish with no questions asked, this may not be ideal, as you may be taking a fish home that could cause you problems. Do your research, initiate a conversation and make your decision afterwards.

The one thing about fishkeeping that's a certainty is that there'll always be more of that species available, either from the same shop or from another one. Don't compromise on fish whose health is dubious, or whose compatibility is questionable. Just wait.

Dos and don'ts of buying fish

Do
- Make sure that you test your aquarium water before purchasing, and make sure that the filter is ready to take fish.
- Take details of your aquarium dimensions, filtration and water-test results with you.
- Take a list of any fish that you already have.
- Read the labels on the fish tanks in the shop, to make sure that the fish are suitable for your own tank.
- Ask the retailer lots of questions about fish compatibility.

Don't
- Don't take too many fish at once.
- Don't buy fish if you're not sure what they are, or how big they grow.
- Don't buy any fish if your water tests reveal that conditions in your tank aren't quite right.
- Don't buy any new fish if you're treating yours for disease.

Transporting fish

As soon as you've paid for your newly acquired fish and left the store, it's your responsibility to get them home safely.

While they're catching the fish, tell the retailer how long your trip home will be. This should enable them to pack the fish with enough oxygen to last the journey. If packed correctly, fish can be transported in sealed polythene bags for 24 hours or more, though that's very much a job for a professional, and should not be tried at home.

In a bag packed one-third with water and two-thirds with atmospheric air, your fish should be able to survive easily for several hours if they're not packed too heavily in each bag. If packed using one-third water and two-thirds pure oxygen they can go much longer, and some stores will use oxygen as a matter of routine.

Also factor acclimatisation into your journey time, as the fish will spend some time floating in the opened bag once you get them home. To be on the safe side, the whole transportation and acclimatisation of the fish shouldn't take any longer than four hours, meaning that you're safe to travel some distance from your home in order to buy them.

The polythene bags in which you're given the fish will usually be placed into brown paper bags and a bag for carrying. The purpose of the brown paper is to block out the light, hopefully calming the fish, and to offer a small degree of insulation.

Keeping them warm

If you're transporting tropical fish it's vital that you keep them warm. If they're allowed to get cold the fish could become stressed and susceptible to Whitespot; if allowed to get colder still they could die.

The best way to keep fish warm over a long journey is to place the polythene fish bag inside a special polystyrene box, available from aquatic stores. This will insulate them against cold or extreme heat, and will cushion them against bumps and knocks on the way. An average-sized polystyrene box will take 8–12 bags of fish, so it's worth getting hold of one and keeping it in the car when travelling to fish shops. Small boxes are also available that are designed to hold just one bag.

If you don't have a polystyrene box, rap the bag in a towel or a sweatshirt to keep the heat in. If travelling by car the fan heater or air conditioning can be utilised to keep the bag warm, but make sure that it doesn't get too hot as this too can stress the fish. More sinisterly, it can also lower the oxygen level in the water.

Below: Inspect the fish after they have been placed in the polythene bag, checking for any signs of ill health.

Below: For long journeys, oxygen can be injected into the bag.

Above: Another bag is placed over the polythene bag to block out light and calm the fish.

Above: The best way to transport fish is in a polystyrene box, keeping them warm and cushioning them.

Below: Once packed in a box take the newly purchased fish straight home.

Keeping them safe

With the heat taken care of, your next responsibility is to ensure that the fish make it home in one piece. As in all areas of fishkeeping, you must make sure that stress is kept to an absolute minimum. By wrapping the bag in a towel, or placing it in a box, light is also blocked out, which will help to calm the fish. With its insulating properties and its ability to absorb impacts a polystyrene box such as those described above is best of all, and should be placed flat in the boot of the car. Failing that, the bags must be wedged into position or held upright, both to prevent them rolling over and to stop the water splashing around too much.

Medium-sized bags fit quite neatly into the foot-well behind the passenger seat in a car, and medium to large bags can even be held in place using a seat belt. Don't place loose fish bags in the boot of the car as they'll roll and bash into the sides continually on the way home; and don't hang them up in the boot, as they'll sway around and hit the sides, shocking the fish and even killing them.

Five things to do when transporting fish

1 Tell the store how long your journey will be.
2 Put the fish bags into a polystyrene box to keep them warm (if travelling for an hour or more).
3 Keep them dark.
4 Wedge the fish bags firmly into position so that they don't roll.
5 Head straight home.

Introducing fish

Once you get the fish home it's very important that they're introduced to the aquarium carefully. As with transporting them, every measure must be taken to keep stress to a minimum.

Acclimatisation

This is the term applied to introducing the fish to the aquarium, equalising the temperature in the fish bag with that of the aquarium, and mixing the two lots of water. As fish don't make their own heat, they're at the mercy of the water temperature around them, and if the water chemistry is different too they could be stressed and even killed.

The floating bag method

1 Assuming that your fish made the journey home OK, the first step is to turn off the aquarium lights. (Being exposed to bright aquarium lights after the darkness of a brown paper bag or polystyrene box is much the same as someone turning on your bedroom light in the middle of the night. Add to that the unfamiliar surroundings of a new tank, and it won't be doing the fishes' stress levels any good at all.) Open the top of the bag or box, and give the fish a few minutes to adjust from darkness to low room lighting.

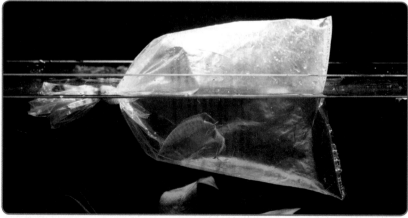

2 Next you need to equalise the water temperature. The most usual method is to float the unopened bag on the surface of the aquarium water. If floating several bags you may need to remove some tank water to allow for displacement by the water in the bags. A typically sized fish bag will take about 20 minutes for the water inside to become equal in temperature to that outside.

Tips for introducing fish

- The fewer fish you add to the system at any one time the better, as the bacteria in the filter will need to grow to catch up with the new fish load. Six fish at any one time is plenty.
- Stress-relieving additives are available for transporting fish. Although not strictly necessary, some liquid products claim to relieve stress while in transport, and can be added either to the bag water at the fish shop, or when the fish are added to the tank once you get them home.
- Although the normal practice is to place newly bought fish straight into the home aquarium, a period of quarantine in a separate tank is by far the better option. See page 123 on why and how to quarantine.

3 Open the bags by untying the rubber band or cutting the knot off. Once open, roll the sides of the bag down, so that it floats on the surface. Introduce some tank water – about a cupful – and leave. Repeat the process every few minutes over the next 20 minutes until the water in the bag is mostly that from the tank. The result will be that the fish are now swimming in water of the same temperature, and same chemistry, as that of the main tank.

4 Introduce the fish by using a small a net to catch them from the floating bag one by one and place them into the main tank.

5 Discard the water in the fish bag, as it will contain ammonia generated by the fish while in transport.

6 Observe the fish in the dark, making sure that they're swimming normally and aren't being attacked by their new tank-mates. If they are being attacked and look visibly distressed, catch the fish with a net, isolate them either in another tank if you have one, or the bag that they were transported in and notify the fish shop straight away as you may have incompatible fish species, and will need to take them back to where you bought them as soon as possible. If they make for the cover at the back of the tank, don't worry, as this is normal behaviour for a fish in unfamiliar surroundings. Only investigate if they remain in hiding for more than a few days.

7 After an hour of being in their new tank, turn the lights back on and check on them every hour or so for the rest of the day.

The drip method

Using an airline, water from the main tank can be dripped very slowly into the open fish bags as they stand in an empty bucket. This process is particularly effective for sensitive species, and is widely used when introducing marine fish and invertebrates. For full step-by-step details see pages 164–5.

Coldwater fish profiles

Comet

Scientific name	Carassius auratus var.
Origin	China.
Size	Up to 30cm, though usually smaller.
Tank size	120cm minimum, though 180cm or outdoor pond is better.
Tank type	Single-tailed goldfish community.
Water conditions	4–30°C, pH 6.5–8.5.
Ease of keeping	Easy.
Swimming level	All levels.
Feeding	Omnivore, feed on flake, pellets, and frozen and live foods.
Breeding	Can be bred, with females becoming plump and males developing breeding tubercles on gill plates and pectoral fins. Egg-scatterer.
Special requirements	Space, efficient filtration.

Notes – Comets are more slender varieties of common goldfish, and with long fins. They can be kept with common goldfish and other single-tailed goldfish varieties, though due to their large size they're better off in an outdoor pond. Usually available in orange. A red-and-white variety called Sarasa is also commonly available.

Black Telescope

Scientific name	Carassius auratus var.
Origin	China.
Size	Around 15cm when adult.
Tank size	90cm and above.
Tank type	Coldwater fancy goldfish community.
Water conditions	15–25°C, pH 7–8.
Ease of keeping	Moderate.
Swimming level	All levels.
Feeding	Omnivore, feed on sinking pellets and granules, frozen and live foods.
Breeding	Can be bred, males developing breeding tubercles on head, gills and pectoral fins. Females become plumper. Egg-scatterer.
Special requirements	Other fancy goldfish for tank-mates, smooth decor.

Notes – Once known as Black Moors, Telescopes are also available in red and calico varieties. Their bulbous eyes add to their appeal, and they're available in both fantail and veil-tailed varieties. They often turn more bronze as they age, and old specimens are prone to cataracts.

Oranda

Scientific name	*Carassius auratus* var.
Origin	China.
Size	Up to 45cm, though usually much smaller at around 15cm.
Tank size	90cm minimum.
Tank type	Coldwater fancy goldfish community.
Water conditions	15–25°C, pH 7–8.
Ease of keeping	Moderate.
Swimming level	All levels.
Feeding	Omnivore, feed on sinking pellets and granules, frozen and live foods.
Breeding	Can be bred, the males developing breeding tubercles on the head, gill covers and pectoral fins, and females becoming plumper. Egg-scatterer.
Special requirements	Other fancy goldfish for tank-mates, smooth decor.

Notes – Orandas are known for their large head growths, which are described by novices as looking like a brain on the outside of their heads. Short-bodied Orandas are prone to buoyancy problems, so feed only sinking foods to overcome this.

Lionhead, Ranchu

Scientific name	*Carassius auratus* var.
Origin	China.
Size	Around 15cm when adult.
Tank size	90cm minimum.
Tank type	Fancy goldfish community.
Water conditions	15–25°C, pH 7–8.
Ease of keeping	Moderate.
Swimming level	All levels.
Feeding	Omnivore, feed on sinking pellets and granules, frozen and live foods.
Breeding	Can be bred, males developing breeding tubercles on the head, gill covers and pectoral fins. Females become plumper. Egg-scatterer.
Special requirements	Other fancy goldfish for tank-mates, smooth decor.

Notes – Lionheads look like Orandas, only without a dorsal fin. They also have short fantails, and aren't very agile swimmers. Available in many colours and varying in quality, show-grade Lionheads are very valuable.

Common Goldfish

Scientific name	*Carassius auratus.*
Origin	China.
Size	Up to 30cm, though usually smaller.
Tank size	Minimum 120cm, though 180cm tank or outdoor pond is best long-term.
Tank type	Coldwater goldfish community.
Water conditions	4–30°C, pH 6.5–8.5.
Ease of keeping	Easy.
Swimming level	All levels.
Feeding	Omnivore, feed on flake, pellets, and frozen and live foods.
Breeding	Can be bred, with females becoming plump and males developing breeding tubercles on gill plates and pectoral fins. Egg-scatterer.
Special requirements	Space and ample filtration.

Notes – Perhaps the most common domestic strain of fish in the world, it could also be the most abused. Often kept in bowls or given away as prizes at the fair, it will do far better in a large coldwater aquarium or outside pond. Keep with members of its own kind.

Fantail, Ryukin

Scientific name	*Carassius auratus var.*
Origin	China.
Size	Around 15cm when adult.
Tank size	90cm minimum.
Tank type	Coldwater fancy goldfish community.
Water conditions	15–25°C, pH 7–8.
Ease of keeping	Moderate.
Swimming level	All levels.
Feeding	Omnivore, feed on sinking pellets and granules, frozen and live foods.
Breeding	Can be bred, males developing breeding tubercles on the head, gill covers and pectoral fins. Females become plumper. Egg-scatterer.
Special requirements	Other fancy goldfish for tank-mates, smooth decor.

Notes – Fantails can become very deep-bodied as they mature, making them susceptible to buoyancy problems. Available in many colours, though red and white are the most common. Fantails don't develop any head growth, making them distinguishable from Orandas when mature.

Pearlscale

Scientific name	*Carassius auratus var.*
Origin	China.
Size	10cm.
Tank size	90cm minimum.
Tank type	Fancy goldfish community.
Water conditions	15–25°C, pH 7–8.
Ease of keeping	Moderate.
Swimming level	All levels.
Feeding	Omnivore, feed on sinking pellets and granules, frozen and live foods.
Breeding	Can be bred, males developing breeding tubercles on the head, gill covers and pectoral fins. Females become plumper. Egg-scatterer.
Special requirements	Other fancy goldfish as tank-mates, smooth decor, slow water flow.

Notes – So-called because of their raised scales, Pearlscales have a spherical body shape and short fins, making them poor swimmers. Prone to buoyancy problems, many Pearlscales resort to a life of sitting on the bottom, so make sure you choose an active one that can swim well. Crown Pearlscales are available, which develop a large bubble on the top of the head as they mature.

Bubble Eye

Scientific name	*Carassius auratus var.*
Origin	China.
Size	15cm.
Tank size	90cm minimum.
Tank type	Single-species coldwater community.
Water conditions	15–25°C pH 7–8.
Ease of keeping	Moderate.
Swimming level	All levels.
Feeding	Omnivore, feed on sinking pellets and granules, frozen and live foods.
Breeding	Can be bred, males developing breeding tubercles on the head, gill covers and pectoral fins. Females become plumper. Egg-scatterer.
Special requirements	Other Bubble Eyes only, room to move, smooth decor or no decor at all.

Notes – This is perhaps the most extreme form of man-made fish available, with its fluid-filled sacks hanging under the eyes. The Bubble Eye is a weak fish, a poor swimmer, and vulnerable to its bubbles bursting and becoming infected. It should only be kept with its own kind.

Celestial, Stargazer

Scientific name	*Carassius auratus var.*
Origin	China.
Size	15cm.
Tank size	90cm minimum.
Tank type	Single-species only.
Water conditions	15–25°C, pH 7–8.
Ease of keeping	Moderate.
Swimming level	All levels.
Feeding	Omnivore, feed on sinking pellets and granules, frozen and live foods.
Breeding	Can be bred, males developing breeding tubercles on the head, gill covers and pectoral fins. Females become plumper. Egg-scatterer.
Special requirements	Company of other Celestials, smooth decor or no decor at all.

Notes – Another extreme man-made goldfish, the Celestial is said to have been bred to gaze up at the emperors. The result is a weak fish that struggles to compete with other fancy goldfish varieties. Only combine with its own type or Bubble Eye varieties.

Weather Loach

Scientific name	*Misgurnus anguillicaudatus.*
Origin	Asia.
Size	Up to 30cm.
Tank size	120cm.
Tank type	Coldwater community, but not with fancy goldfish.
Water conditions	5–25°C, pH 7–8.
Ease of keeping	Moderate.
Swimming level	Bottom.
Feeding	Omnivore, feed on sinking pellets and granules, flake, and frozen and live foods. Ensure its food sinks to the bottom of the aquarium.
Breeding	Bred commercially, but not in aquarium. Females are said to get fat with eggs.
Special requirements	Hiding places, bottom foods, and space.

Notes – Weather Loaches get their name from their erratic behaviour when barometric pressure changes. They're active fish that provide something very different for the large unheated aquarium, though they're not suitable to be mixed with fancy goldfish varieties due to their gregarious nature. Hardy once acclimatised, and a group should be kept.

Temperate fish profiles

Paradise Fish

Scientific name	*Macropodus opercularis.*
Origin	China.
Size	7.5cm.
Tank size	100cm and over.
Tank type	Planted temperate.
Water conditions	15–25°C, pH 6–8.
Ease of keeping	Moderate.
Swimming level	Middle to top.
Feeding	Floating flakes, frozen and live foods.
Breeding	Can be bred in the aquarium. The larger, more colourful and more long- finned male and the plumper, drabber female form a pair. The male blows a floating bubble nest at the surface and entices the female over. Aggressive when breeding.
Special requirements	Plants.

Notes – Like the cool water version of the Siamese Fighting Fish, the Paradise Fish can be aggressive and isn't the best choice for a temperate community including small fish. If kept alone it can be kept in smaller aquariums, though a sexed pair needs an aquarium of 100cm and over.

Zebra Danio

Scientific name	*Danio rerio.*
Origin	India, Pakistan, Nepal and Myanmar.
Size	4cm.
Tank size	60cm.
Tank type	Temperate community, tropical community.
Water conditions	18–24°C, pH 6–8.
Ease of keeping	Easy.
Swimming level	Top.
Feeding	Feed floating flakes, live and frozen foods. Feed frequently.
Breeding	Can be bred. Males are slimmer and more colourful, females are larger and plumper. Egg-scatterer that will readily spawn in the aquarium.

Special requirements Company of its own kind, in a shoal of five or more.

Notes – Zebra Danios are one of the hardiest fish available, and they're inexpensive and readily available. The perfect fish for beginners, they're temperature tolerant and perfect for the unheated aquarium. Golden and long-finned varieties are available.

White Cloud Mountain Minnow

Scientific name   *Tanichthys albonubes.*
Origin   China.
Size   4cm.
Tank size   45cm and over.
Tank type   Temperate small fish community.
Water conditions   18–22°C, pH 6–8.
Ease of keeping   Easy.
Swimming level   Middle to top.
Feeding   Feed crumbled floating flakes, frozen and live foods. Feed regularly.
Breeding   Can be bred, and often spawns in the aquarium. Males are smaller and brighter, females are larger and plumper. Egg-scatterer.
Special requirements Small tank-mates, temperate water temperatures.

Notes – White Cloud Mountain Minnows are very hardy fish that are great additions to the unheated aquarium. Their small size means that they can be kept in small aquariums, and they're a very undemanding species. Long-finned and golden varieties are available.

Rosy Barb

Scientific name   *Puntius conchonius.*
Origin   India, Nepal, Pakistan and Afghanistan.
Size   Up to 14cm, though usually no more than 6cm.
Tank size   90cm.
Tank type   Temperate community.
Water conditions   18–22°C, pH 6–8.
Ease of keeping   Easy.
Swimming level   Middle.
Feeding   Omnivore. Feed flakes, granules, tablets, frozen and live foods.
Breeding   Can be bred in the aquarium, the males taking on a red sheen with black fins, and the females becoming larger and plumper. Egg-scatterer.
Special requirements A group, swimming space.

Notes – Rosy Barbs are very hardy fish that are easy to keep. They're available in several varieties including neon and long-finned types, and most domestic strains are now much more colourful than their wild counterparts.

Variatus Platy

Scientific name   *Xiphophorus variatus.*
Origin   Mexico.
Size   7cm.
Tank size   60cm.
Tank type   Temperate community.
Water conditions   15–25°C, pH 7–8.
Ease of keeping   Easy.
Swimming level   Middle to top.
Feeding   Floating flakes, live and frozen foods. Also grazes algae on rocks.
Breeding   Easy to breed, with pregnant females giving birth to live young. Continuous breeder.
Special requirements More females than males to avoid harassment.

Notes – Variatus Platies are a slightly different species to the other platy, *X. maculatus*, and their natural colours and tank-bred colour variants look slightly different too. Available in many strains including hi-fin varieties, the Variatus Platy prefers cooler temperatures.

Florida Flagfish

Scientific name	*Jordanella floridae.*
Origin	Southern USA.
Size	6cm.
Tank size	50cm.
Tank type	Temperate species or temperate community.
Water conditions	18–22°C, pH 7–8.2.
Ease of keeping	Moderate.
Swimming level	Middle to top.
Feeding	Flakes, frozen and live food, tablet foods and vegetable matter.
Breeding	Can be bred, with the female laying eggs over several days. Males are more colourful, and the females have a black blotch in the dorsal fin. Egg-scatterer.
Special requirements	None.

Notes – Florida Flagfish are sometimes referred to as Killifish, though they're not an annual species like some killies. Preferring slightly cooler water, they're a colourful temperate fish, though they can nip fins if they're hungry.

Borneo Sucker

Scientific name	*Beaufortia leveretti.*
Origin	China and Vietnam.
Size	7cm.
Tank size	80cm.
Tank type	Temperate stream biotope.
Water conditions	18–24°C, pH 6–8.
Ease of keeping	Moderate.
Swimming level	Bottom.
Feeding	Algae wafers, tablet foods and algae growing on rocks.
Breeding	Can be bred, though usually accidentally.
Special requirements	Fast-flowing water, pebbles.

Notes – This species, and several *Pseudogastromyzon* and *Sewellia* species that look and behave like it, are adapted to life in an extreme, fast-flowing environment. They need plenty of water flow, large pebbles upon which to graze, and a plentiful supply of algae.

Red Tail Splitfin

Scientific name	*Xenotoca eiseni.*
Origin	Central America.
Size	6cm.
Tank size	90cm.
Tank type	Temperate community.
Water conditions	15–30°C, pH 6–8.
Ease of keeping	Moderate.
Swimming level	Middle.
Feeding	Flakes, live and frozen foods.
Breeding	Can be bred in the aquarium. Livebearer, though not prolific like platies or guppies, and the male uses a different type of modified anal fin for insemination.
Special requirements	More females than males.

Notes – This odd-looking fish develops strong colours as it grows and is certainly something different for the temperate tank. May nip fins, so only keep with short-finned fish.

Barbatus

Scientific name	*Scleromystax barbatus.*
Origin	Coastal Brazil.
Size	10cm.
Tank size	90cm.
Tank type	Temperate community.
Water conditions	18–22°C, pH 6–8.
Ease of keeping	Moderate.
Swimming level	Bottom.
Feeding	Bottom-scavenger, feeding on tablet foods, live and frozen foods.
Breeding	Can be bred in typical Corydoras fashion, with a pair adopting a T-shaped position. Males are more colourful, females are plumper.
Special requirements	Clean substrate, cool temperatures, and company of its own kind.

Notes – Many tropical fishkeepers fail with this species, purely because they keep it too warm. Place a group in a well-filtered, cool aquarium and they're relatively easy to keep. Formerly called *Corydoras barbatus*, it's one of the largest species available.

Ticto Barb

Scientific name	*Puntius ticto.*
Origin	Pakistan, India, Nepal, Sri Lanka and Thailand.
Size	10cm.
Tank size	90cm.
Tank type	Temperate community.
Water conditions	15–22°C, pH 6.5–7.
Ease of keeping	Easy.
Swimming level	Middle.
Feeding	Flakes, granules, tablets, and frozen and live foods.
Breeding	Can be bred, the males being smaller and more colourful, and the females less colourful, larger and plumper. Egg-scatterer.
Special requirements	Other members of its own kind.

Notes – Ticto Barbs are often overlooked in favour of more colourful species, though there's a variant called the Odessa Barb which is very colourful and would make a great addition to the temperate community tank.

Tropical fish profiles

Barbs and Rasboras

Barbs and Rasboras are popular aquarium fish that have been available to hobbyists for a long time. Varying in size, temperament and colour, there are literally hundreds of species that are well suited to the community aquarium, and many are the mainstay of the tropical fish hobby. Mainly swimming in the middle layers, they should be kept in groups in well-decorated, established aquariums where they'll mature, show off their colours and may even breed. They're easy to feed and generally undemanding.

Harlequin

Scientific name	*Trigonostigma heteromorpha*.
Origin	Thailand, Sumatra and Indonesia.
Size	5cm.
Tank size	60cm.
Tank type	Tropical community.
Water conditions	22–28°C, pH 6–7.5.
Ease of keeping	Easy.
Swimming level	Middle.
Feeding	Flake, frozen and live foods.
Breeding	Can be bred, though not commonly bred in the aquarium. Males have a more pronounced black 'wedge' on the flank, females are larger. Egg-depositor, laying eggs on the underside of a leaf.
Special requirements	Groups, mature aquariums with peaceful fish.

Notes – Harlequins are great fish for the community, that are generally easy to keep and very peaceful. They need to be kept in groups, in mature aquariums, and look great when added in quantity to a planted aquarium. Black Harlequins are available, a tank-bred colour morph, and similar species include its close relatives *T. espei* and *T. hengeli*.

Tiger Barb

Scientific name	*Puntius tetrazona*.
Origin	Sumatra and Borneo.
Size	7cm.
Tank size	90cm.
Tank type	Tropical community with no long-finned fish.
Water conditions	20–28°C, pH 6–8.
Ease of keeping	Moderate.
Swimming level	Middle.
Feeding	Flake, frozen and live foods.
Breeding	Can be bred in the aquarium, though is usually commercially bred in the Far East. Males are more colourful and smaller, females are larger and plumper. Egg-scatterer.
Special requirements	Large groups.

Notes – Tiger Barbs are iconic tropical fish, though their reputation as fin-nippers precedes them. To avoid this undesirable tendency, stock large groups, keep them well fed, give them plenty of swimming space and don't combine them with any long-finned fish. Colour variants including green and albino are readily available.

Denisonii Barb, Red Line Torpedo Barb

Scientific name	Puntius denisonii.
Origin	India.
Size	15cm.
Tank size	120cm minimum.
Tank type	Tropical community.
Water conditions	20–25°C, pH 6.5–8.
Ease of keeping	Moderate.
Swimming level	Middle.
Feeding	Flake, frozen and live foods.
Breeding	Can be bred in the aquarium, though is only just being bred commercially in the Far East, and most aquarium spawnings are accidental. Males are smaller and brighter, females are larger and plumper.
Special requirements	Well-oxygenated water, a group.

Notes – Denisonii Barbs are very popular fish because of their bright colours and peaceful disposition, though they're also quite expensive. They need a large aquarium and plenty of open space for swimming.

Cherry Barb

Scientific name	Puntius titteya.
Origin	Sri Lanka.
Size	5cm.
Tank size	60cm.
Tank type	Tropical community.
Water conditions	23–28°C, pH 6–8.
Ease of keeping	Easy.
Swimming level	Middle.
Feeding	Flake, frozen and live foods.
Breeding	Can be bred in the aquarium. Males turn bright red, while females maintain a brown and cream horizontally striped pattern. Egg-scatterer.
Special requirements	Groups.

Notes – Cherry Barbs are perfect additions to the community of small fish. They're easy to keep, quickly become more colourful, and can be bred quite easily too. Often overlooked in the aquatic shop, add these small fish to a mature, planted aquarium and the males will soon be some of the brightest fish in there.

Golden Barb

Scientific name	Puntius semifasciolatus.
Origin	China.
Size	7cm.
Tank size	90cm.
Tank type	Tropical community.
Water conditions	18–24°C, pH 6–8.
Ease of keeping	Easy.
Swimming level	Middle.
Feeding	Flake, frozen and live foods.
Breeding	Can be bred in the aquarium. The males have more black markings on their bodies, and the females are larger and plumper. Egg-scatterer
Special requirements	Groups.

Notes – Golden Barbs are the domestic form of the Chinese Barb, which is normally pale green in colour. They're hardy, colourful and easy to keep, and quickly mature into stunning, well-behaved fish. They can even be kept in temperate aquariums.

Catfish

Catfish are a diverse group of mainly nocturnal, bottom-scavenging, predatory fish. They vary in size, shape and behaviour greatly, and many catfish are very popular aquarium fish. We use several species to our advantage, as they're known for eating uneaten food off the bottom that's fallen past middle and surface feeders, and many sucker-mouthed species also graze and remove algae from all surfaces, making them great friends of the fishkeeper. Here are just a few examples of this very interesting group.

Corydoras

Scientific name	*Corydoras* and *Scleromystax spp.*
Origin	South America.
Size	Up to 8cm.
Tank size	60cm minimum for a group of smaller species.
Tank type	Tropical community.
Water conditions	20–28°C, pH 6–7.5.
Ease of keeping	Moderate.
Swimming level	Bottom.
Feeding	Sinking tablet and wafers, granules, frozen and live foods.
Breeding	Can be bred in the aquarium. Males are usually smaller with longer dorsal fins. Females are larger and plumper. A pair adopt a T-shaped position in the water, and eggs are often deposited on the aquarium glass.
Special requirements	Groups, soft sand on the bottom.

Notes – Corydoras are perfect catfish for the aquarium as they're very peaceful, stay small and help clear up uneaten food. There are many species available and all can be kept in a similar way. Make sure that the substrate is kept clean, soft enough and fine enough for them to use their delicate barbules to sift through.

Synodontis Catfish

Scientific name	*Synodontis spp.*
Origin	Africa.
Size	Up to 45cm, though usually around 20cm, depending on species.
Tank size	Up to 180cm or more, though 120cm minimum for most species.
Tank type	Large tropical community
Water conditions	Temp 22–28°C, pH 6–8.
Ease of keeping	Moderate.
Swimming level	Bottom.
Feeding	Sinking granules, tablets and pellets, frozen and live foods.
Breeding	Few Synodontis naturally breed in the aquarium, with the exception of *S. multipunctatus* from Lake Tanganyika. Most are bred commercially using hormones or are taken from the wild. Egg-scatterer.
Special requirements	Large aquarium, shady retreats.

Notes – Synodontis are great survivors, as they're hardy and tough enough to be kept with large, boisterous fish like cichlids and oddballs. They're shoaling fish in the wild and mainly nocturnal, though they can be argumentative in the confines of the aquarium. Also known as Upside-down Catfish from the peculiar fashion in which they swim, they're not to be trusted with small fish, as they'll eat them.

Midget Sucker Catfish

Scientific name	Otocinclus spp.
Origin	South America.
Size	3cm.
Tank size	45cm.
Tank type	Tropical community.
Water conditions	24–28°C, pH 6–7.5.
Ease of keeping	Moderate.
Swimming level	Bottom.
Feeding	Sinking tablets, algae wafer, algae.
Breeding	Otocinclus are rarely bred in the aquarium or commercially, and most are taken from the wild. Males are smaller with more markings, females are larger and plumper.
Special requirements	Groups, algae-based foods.

Notes – Otocinclus are great algae eaters for the planted tank, the small community tank or the nano tank, though it must be noted that they're partial to eating the leaves of Amazon Sword plants. Because they're so tiny, a large group can be added to deal with an algae problem, and they can be kept with very small fish.

Bristlenose Catfish

Scientific name	Ancistrus spp.
Origin	Amazon River basin.
Size	15cm.
Tank size	90cm.
Tank type	Tropical community.
Water conditions	22–28°C, pH 6–8.
Ease of keeping	Moderate.
Swimming level	Bottom.
Feeding	Tablet, algae wafer and other sinking foods. Vegetable matter such as cucumber.
Breeding	Can be bred in the aquarium. Males are larger with prominent bristles on the head. Females are shorter and plumper with no bristles. Cave-spawning egg-depositor.

Special requirements An algae-based diet, retreats.

Notes – Bristlenose are hardy fish and are very popular as algae eaters in the aquarium. Groups can be kept, and because they don't grow too large they're a much better choice than larger, more destructive species. Adult pairs will often breed in the community aquarium, and most stores are keen to take in juveniles, which they can sell on.

Pictus Catfish

Scientific name	Pimelodus pictus.
Origin	Amazon and Orinoco River basins.
Size	11cm.
Tank size	120cm.
Tank type	Tropical community with no small fish.
Water conditions	22–28°C, pH 6–8.
Ease of keeping	Moderate.
Swimming level	Bottom.
Feeding	Flake, frozen and live foods.
Breeding	Has not been bred in the aquarium. No sexual differences, and aquarium conditions don't seem to stimulate breeding. Most if not all Pictus are taken from the wild.
Special requirements	Groups.

Notes – Pictus are beautiful shoaling catfish that are always active, though they do have one small problem in that they're adapted to eat small fish. Don't mix any long-whiskered catfish with fish small enough to fit into their mouths, and P. pictus is no exception. Looks good in large shoals in a tank with plenty of water flow.

Striped Dora, Striped Raphael

Scientific name	*Platydoras armatulatus.*
Origin	South America.
Size	25cm.
Tank size	150cm and above.
Tank type	Community with medium to large fish.
Water conditions	24–30°C, pH 6–7.5.
Ease of keeping	Moderate.
Swimming level	Bottom.
Feeding	Sinking pellets and tablets, frozen foods.
Breeding	Has not been bred in the aquarium or commercially. All specimens are taken from the wild and sexual differences are unknown.
Special requirements	Dark places to hide, sinking foods.

Notes – Striped Doras are popular fish when small as they look like humbugs, and become really active at feeding time. In the aquarium they become duller in colour and more nocturnal as they get older and grow larger. They may also eat small fish at night. Added by many as a solution to a snail problem (as they're said to eat them), they're only really suitable for large aquariums with lots of hiding places.

Banjo Catfish

Scientific name	*Platystacus cotylephorus.*
Origin	Venezuela and Brazil.
Size	10cm.
Tank size	75cm and above.
Tank type	South American biotope aquarium or tropical community with small fish.
Water conditions	24–28°C, pH 6–7.5.
Ease of keeping	Moderate.
Swimming level	Bottom.
Feeding	Sinking pellets, frozen and live foods.
Breeding	Has not been bred in the aquarium. Sexual differences are unknown.
Special requirements	Soft sand, small peaceful tank-mates.

Notes – Banjo Catfish are odd-looking fish that like to hide in soft sand, amongst leaf litter and bogwood. They don't swim around in order to find food so shouldn't be kept with fish that may out-compete them at feeding time. Feed mainly on frozen foods like bloodworm and place the food in front of their noses. Biotope tanks are best.

Twig Catfish

Scientific name	*Farlowella vittata.*
Origin	South America.
Size	20cm.
Tank size	120cm.
Tank type	South American biotope or tropical community with small peaceful fish.
Water conditions	24–28°C, pH 6–7.
Ease of keeping	Moderate.
Swimming level	Bottom.
Feeding	Algae, vegetable matter, sinking foods, and tablets.
Breeding	Can be bred in the aquarium, though rarely. Males are larger with bristles on the edge of their nose. Females are smaller, though become plump with eggs. Egg-depositor.

Special requirements Soft water, space, and peaceful tank-mates.

Notes – Twig Catfish demonstrate perfectly just how varied catfish can be. You can see by their camouflage that they'd blend right into a woody environment in the wild. Offer them consistently good water quality and make sure that they get enough food. Don't combine with boisterous fish.

Glass Catfish

Scientific name	*Kryptopterus bicirrhis.*
Origin	Sumatra and Borneo.
Size	10cm.
Tank size	90cm.
Tank type	Tropical community with small fish.
Water conditions	22–26°C, pH 6.5–7.5.
Ease of keeping	Moderate.
Swimming level	Middle.
Feeding	Small frozen and live foods, flakes.
Breeding	Has not been bred in the aquarium.
Special requirements	Shoals.

Notes – Glass Catfish are strange-looking fish that are so-named because you can see right through them. They're constantly active and need to be kept in large groups, in tanks with some water movement. Don't combine with large or boisterous fish, as these catfish are delicate.

Zebra Plec

Scientific name	*Hypancistrus zebra.*
Origin	Rio Xingu, Brazil.
Size	6cm.
Tank size	60cm and above.
Tank type	Tropical community or South American biotope.
Water conditions	23–26°C, pH 6–7.5.
Ease of keeping	Difficult.
Swimming level	Bottom.
Feeding	Sinking foods, tablets, and frozen foods.
Breeding	Can be bred in the aquarium, with the eggs being deposited in caves and the males defending them. Males are larger and more aggressive.
Special requirements	Caves, perfect water quality, and the right food.

Notes – Zebra Plecs were heavily overfished for the aquarium trade at the end of the 20th century, and an export ban was put in place. This caused the price of captive fish to rocket and for people to put a lot of effort into breeding them. They're a stunning catfish, though not one for the beginner as they're aggressive with each other and may get lost in a general community of more competitive fish. Their natural habitat is now further threatened by damming on the Xingu River.

Cichlids

Cichlids are a fascinating group of tropical fish that range greatly in size and behaviour. One feature that is common to all cichlids however is that the parents practice parental care. This evolutionary leap ensures better survival for their young, and cichlids in general do seem to have more intelligence than the average fish, and are hugely popular because of their breeding strategies and behaviour.

Angelfish

Scientific name   Pterophyllum scalare.
Origin: Amazon basin, South America
Size   10cm.
Tank size   120cm.
Tank type   Tropical community.
Water conditions   24–28°C, pH 6–8.
Ease of keeping   Moderate.
Swimming level   Middle.
Feeding   Flakes, frozen and live foods.
Breeding   Can be bred in the aquarium, though adults are often impossible to sex. Domestic forms of Angelfish are poor parents, often eating the eggs as soon as they lay them. Wild Angelfish stand a much better chance of rearing their own eggs. Pair-forming egg-depositor, usually laying them on a vertical surface.
Special requirements A tall tank.

Notes – Angelfish are popular the world over and although there are only three wild species, there are hundreds of aquarium colour variants; you can even get long-finned Angels. Although they may look and behave angelically when they're small, Angels behave much more like cichlids when they're mature, becoming territorial and predatory towards small fish like Neon Tetras.

Severum

Scientific name   Heros spp.
Origin   Amazon River basin.
Size   15cm.
Tank size   150cm.
Tank type   Large tropical community.
Water conditions   24–30°C, pH 6–7.
Ease of keeping   Moderate.
Swimming level   All levels.
Feeding   Flakes, tablets, sticks, pellets, algae wafers, frozen and live foods. Eats plants.
Breeding   Can be bred in the aquarium, the male developing a squiggle pattern on the cheeks whereas the female's face is plain. Pair-forming egg-depositors, choosing rocks or wood upon which to lay. Eggs and fry are protected.
Special requirements A large aquarium, large but peaceful tank-mates.

Notes – Severums are large, peaceful South American cichlids that are straightforward to keep. A popular golden form is available, along with occasional wild regional variants. Severums need large aquariums with sturdy decoration, ideally bogwood, which replicates their natural environment. Feed a diet that is high in vegetable matter and don't include plants in the tank, as they'll eat them.

Discus

Scientific name	*Symphysodon spp.*
Origin	Amazon River basin.
Size	15cm.
Tank size	120cm.
Tank type	Soft-water tropical community or single-species.
Water conditions	26–32°C, pH 5–7.
Ease of keeping	Difficult.
Swimming level	Middle.
Feeding	Granules, frozen and live foods.
Breeding	Can be bred, though often impossible to sex. A pair forms and deposits eggs on a vertical structure. The fry eat mucus from the bodies of the parents after becoming free-swimming.
Special requirements	Soft acidic water, frequent feeding, a tall aquarium and groups

Notes – Discus are special fish that have a following all of their own. They're majestic cichlids that require exacting water parameters and lots of good food. Failure to put them first will result in them turning black and looking unwell. Tank-bred varieties are much hardier than wild fish and easier to keep. There are thought to be three wild species.

Ram

Scientific name	*Mikrogeophagus ramirezi.*
Origin	Venezuela and Columbia.
Size	5cm.
Tank size	60cm.
Tank type	Soft-water tropical community.
Water conditions	24–30°C, pH 6–7.
Ease of keeping	Moderate.
Swimming level	Middle.
Feeding	Flakes, frozen and live foods.
Breeding	Can be bred in the aquarium. The male is larger and more colourful with extended dorsal fin rays. The female is smaller with a round, pink belly. A pit is dug in the substrate or eggs are laid directly onto decor. Egg-depositor.

Special requirements Soft water, a well-decorated mature aquarium.

Notes – Rams are one of the most beautiful tropical freshwater fish and are very popular. They require mature aquariums and soft, acidic water, however, and aren't suitable for beginners. Keep them in pairs, with other small soft-water fish.

Kribensis

Scientific name	*Pelvicachromis pulcher.*
Origin	Southern Nigeria and Cameroon.
Size	10cm.
Tank size	90cm.
Tank type	Tropical community.
Water conditions	24–28°C, pH 6–8.
Ease of keeping	Easy.
Swimming level	Middle to bottom.
Feeding	Flakes, frozen and live foods.
Breeding	Can be bred in the aquarium, the male being larger and longer, and the female developing a pink belly. Pair-forming cave spawners. Eggs are deposited inside, and the parents protect the eggs and fry.
Special requirements	Caves, pairs.

Notes – Kribs are one of the most suitable cichlids for beginners, and their brood-care demonstrates perfectly why people are so attracted to keeping cichlids. More unusual Kribs are also available, including *P. taeniatus*, a very colourful close relative.

Oscar

Scientific name	*Astronotus ocellatus*.
Origin	Amazon River basin.
Size	35cm.
Tank size	180cm.
Tank type	Very large tropical community or single-species.
Water conditions	24–30°C, pH 6–8.
Ease of keeping	Moderate.
Swimming level	All levels.
Feeding	Pellets, sticks, fish, shellfish, earthworms, and large frozen and live foods.
Breeding	Can be bred in the aquarium though rarely is. Commercially bred in the Far East, though they're almost impossible to sex. All-female pairs are common in the aquarium.
Special requirements	Large aquarium, heavy filtration.

Notes – Oscars are large 'pet' fish that beg to their owners for food, and can make life awkward for tank-mates. Grow them up together in order to achieve a pair, and only combine with robust fish such as armoured catfish like Bristlenose catfish and their larger relatives. Powerful filtration is necessary to deal with their waste.

Jewel Cichlid

Scientific name	*Hemichromis spp*.
Origin	West Africa.
Size	Up to 15cm, though usually much smaller.
Tank size	90cm.
Tank type	Large tropical community or single-species.
Water conditions	21–28°C, pH 6.5–7.5.
Ease of keeping	Moderate.
Swimming level	All levels.
Feeding	Flakes, pellets, sticks, and frozen and live foods.
Breeding	Can be bred in the aquarium, with a pair forming and tending the brood. Males are longer with slightly longer fins and mature females take on a rectangular shape around the belly region and vent. Egg-depositor.
Special requirements	Tough tank-mates, pairs.

Notes – Jewel Cichlids are common in aquatic shops though they make a poor choice for the community tank. They can be aggressive and predatory towards small fish, so should only be combined with other non-cichlids that are larger than them. Several species are commonly available, and they're easy to breed.

Yellow Labidochromis

Scientific name	Labidochromis caeruleus 'yellow'.
Origin	Lake Malawi, East Africa.
Size	12cm.
Tank size	120cm.
Tank type	Malawi cichlid community or single-species.
Water conditions	24–28°C, pH 7.5–8.5.
Ease of keeping	Moderate.
Swimming level	All levels.
Feeding	Flake, vegetable matter, pellets, sticks, and some frozen and live foods.
Breeding	Can be bred in aquarium, female holding eggs / fry in her mouth. Males larger with black edges to fins. Females plumper with white belly. No pair bond is formed.
Special requirements	A Malawi cichlid community tank, hard alkaline water, rocks.

Notes – Yellow Labidochromis are bright, pretty cichlids that should only be kept with similar Malawi cichlids in a large, rocky tank set up especially for them. They need to be overcrowded so that hyper-dominant males don't terrorise females and subdominant males and kill them. However, as Malawi cichlids go, Yellow Labs are some of the most peaceful ones.

Fairy Cichlid

Scientific name	Neolamprologus pulcher.
Origin	Lake Tanganyika, East Africa.
Size	7cm.
Tank size	90cm.
Tank type	Tanganyikan cichlid community or single-species.
Water conditions	24–28°C, pH 7.5–8.5.
Ease of keeping	Moderate.
Swimming level	Bottom to middle.
Feeding	Flake, frozen and live foods.
Breeding	Very prolific breeder, with several generations of same family combining to form a super-family. Difficult to sex, and pairs best left to decide their own mates out of a group. Cave-spawning egg-depositor.

Special requirements Hard alkaline water, a rocky tank.

Notes – Brichardi are easy to breed, though once they've started they rarely stop, and as the family grows tank-mates are tolerated less and less. An interesting breeding project for those wanting to breed their first cichlid, though few people will rehome the youngsters if you become overrun.

Convict Cichlid

Scientific name	Amatitlania nigrofasciata.
Origin	Central America.
Size	10cm.
Tank size	90cm.
Tank type	Large tropical community, cichlid community or single-species.
Water conditions	24–30°C, pH 7–8.
Ease of keeping	Moderate.
Swimming level	Middle to bottom.
Feeding	Flakes, pellets, and frozen and live foods.
Breeding	Very prolific breeder. Males are larger with longer fins, and females develop a colourful area on the belly. Pair-forming cave spawner that aggressively defends its brood. Egg-depositor.
Special requirements	Caves, pairs, and tough tank-mates.

Notes – Convict Cichlids are hardy cichlids that are very easy to breed, though that's also their downfall. If a pair is placed into a community they quickly spawn and then terrorise their tank-mates as they try to herd their fry around the aquarium and find food. They're so prolific that many shops won't rehome their offspring and they're largely worthless.

Firemouth

Scientific name	*Thorichthys meeki.*
Origin	Yucatan, Mexico, Belize and Guatemala.
Size	15cm.
Tank size	100cm.
Tank type	Community aquarium with medium to large fish.
Water conditions	26–30°C, pH 6.5–7.5.
Ease of keeping	Moderate.
Swimming level	Middle to bottom.
Feeding	Flakes, pellets, sticks, frozen and live foods.
Breeding	Can be bred in the aquarium, with a pair forming, depositing eggs and defending the brood. Males are slightly larger and more colourful, with longer fins.

Special requirements Rocks, wood and gravel in which to find food, space.

Notes – Firemouths are popular cichlids, but have declined in popularity as hobbyists have opted more for African lake cichlids over Central Americans. Once mature they can become very colourful, with red throats and grey body taking on a red sheen. They do lots of gill flaring when defending territory, though they're one of the most peaceful Central American cichlids.

Venustus

Scientific name	*Nimbochromis venustus.*
Origin	Lake Malawi, East Africa.
Size	Up to 30cm.
Tank size	180cm.
Tank type	Lake Malawi cichlid tank.
Water conditions	25–27°C, pH 7.5–8.5.
Ease of keeping	Moderate.
Swimming level	All levels.
Feeding	Flakes, pellets, sticks, frozen fish and shellfish.
Breeding	Can be bred in the aquarium, with the female brooding the young in her mouth. Males are larger and more colourful, females retain the giraffe pattern.
Special requirements	Space, no small tank-mates.

Notes – Venustus are popular cichlids for the Lake Malawi cichlid aquarium as they're generally hardy and have a different shape and pattern to the Mbuna. There's a slight issue with Venustus, however, as in Lake Malawi they're predators of small cichlids and are quite capable of eating immature cichlids in the aquarium. Best kept in a large, open Malawi tank with other similar species, and fed on a fishy diet.

Congo Lumphead, Blockhead Cichlid

Scientific name	*Steatocranus casuarius.*
Origin	Congo River basin, Africa.
Size	10cm.
Tank size	90cm.
Tank type	African river biotope or tropical community with medium-sized fish.
Water conditions	24–28°C, pH 6–8.
Ease of keeping	Moderate.
Swimming level	Bottom.
Feeding	Flakes, live and frozen foods.
Breeding	Can be bred in aquarium, with a pair forming and depositing eggs in a cave, where they defend eggs and young. Males larger, with a more pronounced hump on head and longer fins.
Special requirements	Caves and space to make a territory.

Notes – Congo Lumpheads may lack colour but they more than make up for it in character. Inhabiting fast-flowing rocky rivers in the wild, they need a suitably rocky aquarium in which to live. Offer the male several females to choose from and combine with fast-moving riverine fish that will stay out of the male's way.

Frontosa

Scientific name	Cyphotilapia frontosa.
Origin	Lake Tanganyika, East Africa.
Size	35cm.
Tank size	180cm.
Tank type	Single-species is best.
Water conditions	24–26°C, pH 8–8.5.
Ease of keeping	Moderate.
Swimming level	Middle to bottom.
Feeding	Pellets, sticks, frozen fish and frozen shellfish.
Breeding	Can be bred in the aquarium, with females protecting the large brood in her mouth. Males are larger with longer fins and a more pronounced hump.
Special requirements	Space, good water quality, low light, peaceful tank-mates or none at all.

Notes – Frontosa are specialised fish that live at depth in Lake Tanganyika. In the aquarium they're slow-moving and shouldn't be combined with boisterous fish, despite their size. Keep them in groups of one male and several females, in large tanks with rocky retreats and subdued lighting.

Jack Dempsey

Scientific name	Rocio octofasciata.
Origin	Mexico and Honduras.
Size	20cm.
Tank size	120cm and above.
Tank type	Cichlid community or tropical community of large fish.
Water conditions	22–30°C, pH 7–8.
Ease of keeping	Moderate.
Swimming level	Middle to bottom.
Feeding	Pellets, sticks, frozen and live foods.
Breeding	Can be bred in aquarium, with a pair forming and depositing eggs in a cave or pit on a hard surface. Males larger, more colourful and develop square head. Females darker with more markings on face.
Special requirements	Space, robust tank-mates.

Notes – Jack Dempseys are good medium-sized Central American cichlids to try keeping, and are generally hardy. For best results don't combine with any other cichlids and offer a large tank decorated with rocks and bogwood. A blue version is also available and is highly desirable, demanding a high price.

Auratus

Scientific name	Melanochromis auratus.
Origin	Lake Malawi, East Africa.
Size	15cm.
Tank size	120cm and above..
Tank type	Lake Malawi Mbuna tank.
Water conditions	24–28°C, pH 7.5–8.5.
Ease of keeping	Moderate.
Swimming level	All levels.
Feeding	Flakes, frozen foods, vegetable matter.
Breeding	Can be bred in aquarium, with female mouthbrooding eggs and fry. No pair bond is formed. Males turn black and white. Females remain more yellow, black and white, like juvenile colouration.
Special requirements	Rocks, space, lots of Mbuna tank-mates to diffuse aggression.

Notes – Auratus are one of the most popular Malawi cichlids and often one of the first to be purchased for a new tank. But they're also one the most aggressive cichlids, and should really be added last, as juveniles, or not at all, in order to keep the peace. Juveniles are stunningly marked, though most become drabber as they get older.

Livebearers

Live bearing fish are fascinating, small, tropical fish that give birth to live young instead of laying eggs. This breeding strategy means that the fry are better equipped to feed and avoid predation as soon as they are born, rather than being at extra risk as eggs. It has also made them very popular as aquarium specimens because they breed readily in the home aquarium and are often the first fish that a hobbyist manages to have breed. As a group, nearly all livebearers are active, small, and easy to keep. Several species are now available in a huge range of ornamental varieties too, adding to their range of colour, and over all appeal.

Molly

Scientific name	*Poecilia latipinna, velifera, sphenops.*
Origin	Central America.
Size	Up to 15cm, though usually much smaller.
Tank size	90cm.
Tank type	Tropical community.
Water conditions	22–28°C, pH 7.5–8.2, also brackish water.
Ease of keeping	Easy.
Swimming level	Middle to top.
Feeding	Flakes, tablets, algae wafers, live and frozen foods. Also grazes algae.
Breeding	Very prolific breeders, with females giving birth to large, live young on a monthly basis. Male Sailfin Mollies have a large dorsal fin, whereas females don't, but they can also be sexed by the spiky anal fin which the male uses for insemination. The female's anal fin is a normal triangular shape.
Special requirements	More females than males, a refuge for females to give birth. Salt in the water.

Notes – Three scientific names have been listed because all three species are available and can be kept in the same way. However, a modern Molly may be a cross combining all three species. *P. latipinna* and *P. velifera* are the original Sailfin Mollies, with *P. sphenops* being the Black Molly. All Mollies benefit from slightly salty water conditions, failing which they need hard alkaline water.

Swordtail

Scientific name	*Xiphophorus hellerii.*
Origin	Central America.
Size	Up to 14cm, though usually much smaller.
Tank size	90cm.
Tank type	Tropical community.
Water conditions	22–28°C, pH 7.5–8.2.
Ease of keeping	Easy.
Swimming level	Middle to top.
Feeding	Flakes, tablets and algae wafers. Also grazes on algae.
Breeding	Very prolific breeder with females giving birth to live young on a monthly basis. Males can be told from the females because they develop the long, sword-like tail extension that gives them their name.
Special requirements	Space to swim, more females than males, and a refuge for the females to give birth.

Notes – Swordtails are popular livebearers available in many different colours and patterns, and even in lyre-tailed, long-finned forms. Give the males plenty of swimming space to encourage the tail to develop to its full potential. Although tales are told of 14cm Swordtails and larger, most modern Swordtails never achieve that size.

Guppy

Scientific name	*Poecilia reticulata.*
Origin	Trinidad, Barbados, Venezuela and Northern Brazil.
Size	Males 3.5cm, females 6cm.
Tank size	45cm.
Tank type	Small fish tropical community.
Water conditions	18–28°C, pH 7–8.
Ease of keeping	Easy.
Swimming level	Top.
Feeding	Floating flakes, live and frozen foods, algae wafers and tablets.
Breeding	Very prolific breeders with mature females giving birth to live young on a monthly basis. Males are small and colourful, with most domestic forms having a large tail. Females are larger and less colourful.

Special requirements More males than females, a refuge for females to give birth.

Notes – Guppies were one of the first tropical fish to be kept and bred commercially, and they're one of the most abundant fish in the world. Many aquarium strains look nothing like the smaller wild guppies, and have much brighter colours and large tails. Due to inbreeding, domestic guppy strains are not very hardy.

Platy

Scientific name	*Xiphophorus maculatus.*
Origin	Mexico and Belize.
Size	Males 4cm, females 6cm.
Tank size	60cm.
Tank type	Tropical community tank.
Water conditions	18–25°C, pH 7–8.
Ease of keeping	Easy.
Swimming level	Middle to top.
Feeding	Flakes, tablets, algae wafers and frozen and live foods.
Breeding	Very prolific breeder, with the female giving birth to live young. Males can be identified by the modified anal fin that looks like a spike, whereas females are larger and become much more plump when they're pregnant.

Special requirements More females than males, a refuge for females to give birth.

Notes – Platies are great fish for beginners as they're easy to keep, easy to breed and very colourful. They're available in hundreds of different pattern and colour combinations, though inbreeding to create these varieties has left them not as hardy as they once were.

Endler's

Scientific name	*Poecilia wingei.*
Origin	Venezuela.
Size	2cm for males, females larger.
Tank size	45cm.
Tank type	Tropical community of small fish.
Water conditions	20–28°C, pH 6.5–8.2.
Ease of keeping	Easy.
Swimming level	Middle to top.
Feeding	Flakes, tablets, algae wafers, and live and frozen foods.
Breeding	Very prolific breeder, with females giving birth to live young on a monthly basis. Females are larger, plain fish, with males being smaller but much more colourful.
Special requirements	More females than males, a refuge for females to give birth.

Notes – Endler's are relative newcomers to the hobby, and look very much like a wild guppy. In the few years that they've been available they've already been line-bred to accentuate their colours and tail shapes, and have also been crossed with guppies, meaning that it's getting harder to purchase true Endler's that aren't guppy crosses.

Bottom dwelling cypriniids

In the same family as barbs, rasboras and even goldfish, these other popular fish behave more like catfish than barbs, hugging the bottom in search for food. They are popular because of their striking colour patterns like the Clown loach or Red tailed black shark, or because of the useful cleaning job that they can do in the aquarium like the Chinese algae eater. Something that they all provide is movement in the bottom layers of the aquarium.

Clown Loach

Scientific name	*Chromobotia macracanthus.*
Origin	Sumatra and Borneo, Indonesia.
Size	30cm.
Tank size	180cm.
Tank type	Large tropical community.
Water conditions	25–30°C, pH 6–8.
Ease of keeping	Moderate.
Swimming level	Bottom.
Feeding	Sinking tablets and granules, frozen and live foods.
Breeding	Accidentally spawned in the aquarium, though usually commercially bred using hormone injections. Sexing is difficult. Females are larger and plumper when full of eggs. Egg-scatterer.
Special requirements	Space, warm water, groups.

Notes – Clown Loach are very striking fish and very popular because of their markings, though they do need to be kept in groups and can grow very large. Provide a large aquarium with good water quality and good food. Whitespot is often brought about by stress and exposure to low temperatures.

Coolie Loach

Scientific name	*Pangio kuhlii.*
Origin	South-East Asia.
Size	12cm.
Tank size	90cm.
Tank type	Tropical community.
Water conditions	24–30°C, pH 6–7.5.
Ease of keeping	Moderate.
Swimming level	Bottom.
Feeding	Sinking tablets, frozen and live foods.
Breeding	Has been accidentally bred in the aquarium. Females become much larger and plumper when full of eggs. Egg-scatterer.
Special requirements	Groups, retreats, and small sinking foods.

Notes – Coolie Loach are popular bottom-scavenging fish that are useful for getting into all the nooks and crannies to find food. Several species are available, all with similar requirements.

Red Tail Black Shark

Scientific name	Epalzeorhynchos bicolor.
Origin	Thailand.
Size	12cm.
Tank size	120cm.
Tank type	Tropical community.
Water conditions	22–26°C, pH 6.5–7.5.
Ease of keeping	Moderate.
Swimming level	Bottom.
Feeding	Sinking tablets and algae wafers, frozen and live foods.
Breeding	Has not been bred in the aquarium, though it is bred commercially using hormones. Females are presumably larger and fuller when carrying eggs. Egg-scatterer.
Special requirements	A large aquarium, retreats.

Notes – Red Tail Black Sharks are stunning fish, if somewhat territorial, and should be the only one of their kind added to an aquarium. They also like to chase bottom-dwelling rivals and fish that are similar in shape or colour to them, so choose tank-mates wisely, and only keep one red tail black shark per tank as they will fight with their own kind. Provide a large, well-decorated tank in order to calm its territorial tendencies.

Chinese Algae Eater

Scientific name	Gyrinocheilus aymonieri.
Origin	Mekong, Chao Phraya and Meklong river basins, South-East Asia.
Size	28cm, usually much smaller.
Tank size	120cm.
Tank type	Tropical community.
Water conditions	24–28°C, pH 6–8.
Ease of keeping	Moderate.
Swimming level	Bottom.
Feeding	Sinking tablets and algae wafers, algae.
Breeding	Has not been bred in the aquarium, though they're commercially bred using hormone injections. Females are larger and plumper. Egg-scatterer.
Special requirements	Large tank, algae, and retreats.

Notes – Chinese Algae Eaters are one of the best algae eaters, busily grazing all decor and the aquarium glass all day long. The only problem is that as they mature they become territorial and aggressive. Golden varieties are available.

Panda Garra

Scientific name	Garra flavatra.
Origin	Myanmar.
Size	6cm.
Tank size	90cm.
Tank type	Tropical community.
Water conditions	24–28°C, pH 6–7.5.
Ease of keeping	Moderate.
Swimming level	Bottom.
Feeding	Sinking tablet and algae wafers, algae.
Breeding	Has not been bred in the aquarium. Sexual differences and spawning habits are unknown.
Special requirements	Fast, well-oxygenated water, algae-based foods.

Notes – Panda Garra are relative newcomers to the hobby. They're very colourful as Garra go, and stay small too, making them popular if somewhat expensive loaches. The ideal set-up would contain a group in a tank set up like a fast-flowing stream. Provide lots of flow and oxygen, which in turn will encourage algae growth.

Oddballs

Oddball is a catch all name for many weird and wonderful fish species that don't belong to the main, popular families of aquarium fish. Oddballs may be kept because of their strange looks or behaviour, and many are quite intelligent species, needing to be clever in order to catch their prey in the wild. With few exceptions, oddball species are not to be kept with small 'community' species like guppies, and should be housed on their own, in a tank set up and arranged specially for them.

Butterflyfish

Scientific name	Pantodon buchholzi.
Origin	Central and West Africa.
Size	11cm.
Tank size	90cm.
Tank type	Single-species, biotope or selected tropical community.
Water conditions	23–30°C, pH 6–7.5.
Ease of keeping	Difficult.
Swimming level	Top.
Feeding	Live insects floating on the surface, some frozen and floating live foods, carnivore sticks.
Breeding	Unknown, all specimens are taken from the wild. Paternal mouthbrooder?
Special requirements	Floating plants, still water, bottom-feeding fish such as small Synodontis that won't clash with their feeding method.

Notes – Butterflyfish are fairly commonly available but aren't suitable for the normal community tank. They're extremely adapted to life at the surface of still waters and swamps, where they eat floating insects. They're actually a small relative of the Arowana, with a similar trapdoor mouth arrangement and excellent jumping skills. In the aquarium they can suffer from fin-nipping and not being fed appropriate foods. They commonly starve to death or jump out as a result.

Mbu Pufferfish

Scientific name	Tetraodon mbu.
Origin	Congo River basin and rivers flowing into Lake Tanganyika, Africa.
Size	75cm.
Tank size	300cm and above.
Tank type	Single-species, biotope aquarium or specially selected community.
Water conditions	24–26°C, pH 6–8.
Ease of keeping	Moderate.
Swimming level	All levels.
Feeding	Crabs, snails and shellfish.
Breeding	Has not been bred in the aquarium or commercially. Sexual differences and breeding method unknown.
Special requirements	Huge aquariums, huge filters, and shellfish in shells.

Notes – Mbu Puffers are also known as Giant Freshwater Puffers, as they can grow to over 60cm in length. Because of this they'll eventually need huge aquariums, but despite this they're frequently sold. They have great character and become pet fish. Puffers have many endearing characteristics including large, moving eyes and comical gazes and swimming action. The Mbu grows quickly and will gorge itself on shellfish until it can't swim. Feed sparingly with whole shellfish every few days. Adequate filtration is a must.

Siamese Tiger Fish

Scientific name	*Datnioides microlepis.*
Origin	Borneo, Sumatra and Thailand.
Size	Up to 45cm, usually smaller.
Tank size	180cm.
Tank type	Oddball community of large fish or single-species tank.
Water conditions	22–26°C, pH 6–8.
Ease of keeping	Moderate.
Swimming level	Middle.
Feeding	Live and frozen foods, fish.
Breeding	Has been bred commercially, but not in the home aquarium. Egg-scatterer? Sexual differences unknown, though females are probably larger.
Special requirements	A large tank, meaty foods.

Notes – A striking predatory fish that carries a high price tag when large. There are several species available, of which *D. microlepis* is the most common and easiest to keep. *D. quadrifasciatus* is brackish. Although large and predatory, Tiger Fish should not be kept with aggressive or boisterous species.

Colomesus Puffer

Scientific name	*Colomesus asellus.*
Origin	Amazon River basin.
Size	Up to 14cm, though usually much smaller.
Tank size	100cm.
Tank type	Single-species.
Water conditions	22–28°C, pH 6–7.5.
Ease of keeping	Moderate.
Swimming level	Middle.
Feeding	Snails, shellfish, carnivore sticks.
Breeding	Has not been bred in the aquarium. Sexual differences unknown.
Special requirements	Snails.

Notes – Colomesus Puffers are true freshwater pufferfish that, unusually for pufferfish, inhabit soft water. They're very active, with sharp beaks, and they can't be trusted not to bite other fish and their fins. One potential problem with this species is overgrowing teeth. A diet of snails and shellfish in their shells must be fed at all times in order to keep the teeth ground down. DIY dental surgery has been effective but isn't recommended. Instead, consult a vet that specialises in fish.

Silver Arowana

Scientific name	*Osteoglossum bicirrhosum.*
Origin	Amazon River basin.
Size	120cm.
Tank size:	500cm and above.
Tank type	Single-species or community of huge fish.
Water conditions	24–30°C, pH 6–7.5.
Ease of keeping	Moderate.
Swimming level	Top.
Feeding	Large insects, frozen and live foods, fish, carnivore sticks.
Breeding	Has been bred commercially, the male tending the brood in his mouth. Mouth brooder. Sexual differences unknown.
Special requirements	Huge aquariums or tropical ponds, overhanging vegetation.

Notes – Silver Arowana belong to a family of large prehistoric fish known as the bony tongues. It has a very distinctive look and its cousin the Asian Arowana is also known as the Dragon Fish. In the wild, Arowana glide into the flooded forest and leap to take insects from tree branches. In captivity few aquariums are large enough to house them long-term and they often develop a condition known as drop-eye, when the eyes turn to permanently face downwards. A tight-fitting cover must be used to prevent them jumping out, though they aren't really suitable for home aquariums at all.

Red-Bellied Piranha

Scientific name	*Pygocentrus nattereri.*
Origin	Amazon River basin.
Size	35cm.
Tank size	180cm.
Tank type	Single-species.
Water conditions	24–28°C, pH 6–7.5.
Ease of keeping	Moderate.
Swimming level	Middle.
Feeding	Meaty frozen foods, fish. Juveniles will eat dry foods.
Breeding	Has been bred occasionally in the aquarium, though not a common occurrence. Males are smaller and more colourful. Females are larger and plumper.
Special requirements	Large aquariums, powerful filtration, large single-species groups.

Notes – Red-Bellied Piranhas are infamous around the world for their feeding frenzies and their ability to tear flesh, but in the aquarium they're a timid species that must be kept in large, similarly-sized groups. Care must be taken when transporting and moving Piranhas or when doing tank maintenance, since although they're shy, serious injuries can be inflicted on human limbs.

Rainbow Snakehead

Scientific name	*Channa bleheri.*
Origin	India.
Size	13cm.
Tank size	100cm.
Tank type	Single-species or oddball community.
Water conditions	20–28°C, pH 6–7.5.
Ease of keeping	Moderate.
Swimming level	All levels.
Feeding	Meaty frozen and live foods, insects, fish.
Breeding	Can be bred in the aquarium, though adults are difficult to sex and most spawnings have been accidental. Mouth brooder.
Special requirements	A tight-fitting lid, retreats.

Notes – Rainbow Snakeheads should fulfil every need that the oddball fishkeeper has. They're predatory, snakelike, and refuse to be tamed. Top that with great colouration and an adult size that won't outgrow a standard tank and you have a very desirable oddball. This species is particularly prone to escaping the confines of the aquarium.

Ornate Bichir

Scientific name	*Polypterus ornatipinnis*.
Origin	Congo River basin, Africa.
Size	60cm.
Tank size	180cm minimum.
Tank type	Single-species or oddball community tank.
Water conditions	24–28°C, pH 6–8.
Ease of keeping	Moderate.
Swimming level	Bottom.
Feeding	Meaty frozen and live foods, earthworms, fish.
Breeding	Can be bred in the aquarium, though rarely is. Males are longer with a modified anal fin, which they use in spawning. Females are shorter, with a shorter anal fin. Egg-scatterer.
Special requirements	Meaty food, retreats.

Notes – Ornate Bichirs are snake-like oddballs that are generally well behaved and sedate. The Ornate is one of the most patterned and colourful *Polypterus* species, with juveniles covered in black and gold markings. Rarely reaches its full size potential.

Motoro Stingray

Scientific name	*Potamotrygon motoro*.
Origin	Amazon River basin.
Size	60cm diameter.
Tank size	180cm x 90cm wide.
Tank type	Large fish community, South American large fish biotope or single-species.
Water conditions	24–26°C, pH 5–7.
Ease of keeping	Difficult.
Swimming level	Bottom.
Feeding	Meaty frozen and live foods, earthworms, fish.
Breeding	Can be bred in aquarium, with larger female giving birth to live young. Can be sexed, as male fish have claspers.
Special requirements	Perfect water quality, large flat tanks, suitable foods and tank-mates.

Notes – Stingrays are totally different to anything that you would normally see available for the tropical fish tank. They're large, flat fish that need an equally large, flat area and soft sand in which to bury themselves. Water quality must be optimum at all times, and fish must be settled and feeding well before they're sold. Not for beginners. The sting in the tail can inflict serious injuries.

Elephant Nose

Scientific name	*Gnathonemus petersii*.
Origin	Niger and Congo River basins, Africa.
Size	35cm.
Tank size	180cm.
Tank type	West African biotope tank or oddball community.
Water conditions	22–28°C, pH 6–8.
Ease of keeping	Difficult.
Swimming level	Bottom.
Feeding	Bloodworms, Tubifex worms, other small live foods. Will not accept dry foods.
Breeding	Has not been bred in the aquarium.
Special requirements	Large dimly-lit aquarium, perfect water quality, small live worms.

Notes – Elephant Nose are popular for their strange look and behaviour, though they're ill suited to life in most aquariums. They grow large and shoal in the wild, but in the confines of the aquarium they often fight and squabble. They're also specialised feeders, adapted to search for live invertebrates in mud. The nearest that we can get to a mud substrate is fine sand, and we often provide insufficient live foods to keep them well-fed and happy. Not for beginners.

Rainbowfish

Rainbowfish are so called because of the beautiful colours displayed by adults, when mature. They come mainly from Australasia and are active, colourful, medium sized community fish that behave much like barbs do. To get the best colours from rainbowfish, stock in a large, well decorated aquarium, and feed a varied diet. Only after a few years of keeping them will you see the best colours, as they are slow to mature.

Red Rainbowfish

Scientific name	Glossolepis incisus.
Origin	Irian Jaya, Indonesia.
Size	12cm.
Tank size	120cm.
Tank type	Tropical community.
Water conditions	22–26°C, pH 7–8.
Ease of keeping	Moderate.
Swimming level	Middle.
Feeding	Flakes, frozen and live foods.
Breeding	Can be bred in the aquarium, and bred commercially. Males are larger and more colourful, females are smaller, plainer in colour and plumper. Egg-scatterer.
Special requirements	Space, good water quality.

Notes – Red Rainbows really stand out, with the male's crimson red colouration and high levels of activity. Rainbows look best when kept together in large planted aquariums, or mixed with other similar fish such as medium-sized barbs. Adults can be too competitive to be mixed with small, timid tropicals.

Boesemani Rainbowfish

Scientific name	Melanotaenia boesemani.
Origin	Irian Jaya, Indonesia.
Size	10cm.
Tank size	100cm.
Tank type	Tropical community.
Water conditions	24–28°C, pH 7–8.
Ease of keeping	Moderate.
Swimming level	Middle.
Feeding	Flakes, frozen and live foods.
Breeding	Can be bred in the aquarium, and is bred commercially. Males are even brighter than females, and the two dorsal fins touch when relaxed. Females are plumper. Egg-scatterer.
Special requirements	Space, good water quality, and good food.

Notes – Few fish can compare with the colours of the Boesemani Rainbowfish. The combination of bright yellow and rich blue make this species deservedly popular, though it takes a lot of time, water-changes and good food to get the best out of this slow-maturing species.

Dwarf Neon Rainbowfish

Scientific name	Melanotaenia praecox.
Origin	Irian Jaya, Indonesia.
Size	5cm.
Tank size	80cm.
Tank type	Tropical community.
Water conditions	22–28°C, pH 6.5–8.
Ease of keeping	Moderate.
Swimming level	Middle.
Feeding	Flakes, frozen and live foods.
Breeding	Can be bred in the aquarium, and is bred commercially. Males are larger with bluer colouration, a deeper body and redder fins. Females are smaller and less colourful. Egg-scatterer.
Special requirements	Good water quality.

Notes – Neon Dwarf Rainbows are almost perfect specimens for the tropical aquarium as they're well-behaved, become more colourful as they mature, and stay small. Keep a group of them with mixed sexes, either in a standard tropical community or a rainbowfish-specific aquarium.

Celebes Rainbowfish

Scientific name	Marosatherina ladigesi.
Origin	Sulawesi, Indonesia.
Size	8cm.
Tank size	80cm.
Tank type	Tropical community.
Water conditions	22–28°C, pH 7–8.
Ease of keeping	Moderate.
Swimming level	Middle.
Feeding	Flakes, frozen and live foods.
Breeding	Can be bred in the aquarium, though usually bred commercially. Males are larger with more colour and longer fins. Females are smaller and plainer. Egg-scatterer.
Special requirements	Good water quality, groups.

Notes – Celebes Rainbowfish are often overlooked in favour of other more colourful species, but their colour and shape is subtly beautiful, and complements the bright green colours of a well-planted tank. The fins become much longer on male fish as they mature, and the yellow becomes almost neon.

Forktail Rainbowfish

Scientific name	Pseudomugil furcatus.
Origin	Papua New Guinea.
Size	5cm.
Tank size	60cm.
Tank type	Tropical community of small fish.
Water conditions	24–26°C, pH 6–8.
Ease of keeping	Moderate.
Swimming level	Middle to top.
Feeding	Flakes, frozen and live foods.
Breeding	Can be bred in the aquarium, though they're usually commercially bred. Males are larger and more colourful, with longer fins. Females are smaller and plainer.
Special requirements	Groups, small peaceful tank-mates.

Notes – Forktail Rainbowfish are colourful little fish with their bright blue eyes and yellow edging to the fins. They look great in large groups in well-planted tanks. Choose shop-bought specimens carefully, as some have spinal deformities.

Tetras

Tetras are some of the most popular aquarium fish, known for their small to medium size, good behaviour and shoaling tendencies. They need mature tanks and peaceful, similarly sized tank-mates. They often group together in mid-water, and most species are best kept in soft to neutral water conditions. Tetras are the perfect complement to Corydoras catfish.

Neon Tetra

Scientific name	*Paracheirodon innesi.*
Origin	Solimoes River, South America.
Size	4cm.
Tank size	45cm.
Tank type	Tropical community of small fish.
Water conditions	20–26°C, pH 6–7.5.
Ease of keeping	Moderate.
Swimming level	Middle.
Feeding	Flakes, frozen and live foods.
Breeding:	Bred commercially, though rarely breeds in the home aquarium. Females are larger and plumper. Males are smaller and brighter. Egg-scatterer.
Special requirements	Groups, small peaceful tank-mates.

Notes – Neon Tetras are one the world's most popular aquarium fish, and are recognisable by hobbyists and non-fishkeepers alike. Keep them in groups in mature aquariums with other small community fish. Whitespot may come about from stress.

Cardinal Tetra

Scientific name	*Paracheirodon axelrodi.*
Origin	Upper Orinoco and Rio Negro rivers, Brazil.
Size	4cm.
Tank size	45cm.
Tank type	Tropical community.
Water conditions	24–30°C, pH 6–7.5.
Ease of keeping	Moderate.
Swimming level	Middle.
Feeding	Flakes, frozen and live foods.
Breeding	Rarely bred in the aquarium, though bred commercially in Europe. Females are larger and plumper. Egg-scatterer.
Special requirements	Warm water, groups.

Notes – Cardinal Tetras are even better-looking than Neon Tetras, with more colour, and because of this they command a higher price. They require warm, soft water and groups of ten or more to feel happy. Whitespot may come about if they're kept in stressful or unsuitable conditions.

Congo Tetra

Scientific name	*Phenacogrammus interruptus*.
Origin	Congo Democratic Republic, Africa.
Size	8cm.
Tank size	100cm.
Tank type	Tropical community.
Water conditions	23–28°C, pH 6–7.5.
Ease of keeping	Moderate.
Swimming level	Middle.
Feeding	Flakes, frozen and live foods.
Breeding	Bred commercially though rarely bred in the aquarium, despite adults spawning frequently. Males are larger and more colourful with dorsal and tail fin extensions. Females are plain, and become plumper. Egg-scatterer.
Special requirements	Groups, a spacious aquarium.

Notes – These are beautiful tetras for the larger aquarium, with the males developing gorgeous colours and fin extensions as they mature. Congo Tetras are quite skittish fish that need the company of their own kind, and a spacious but well-decorated aquarium.

Emperor Tetra

Scientific name	*Nematobrycon palmeri*.
Origin	South America.
Size	4cm.
Tank size	60cm.
Tank type	Tropical community.
Water conditions	23–27°C, pH 6–8.
Ease of keeping	Moderate.
Swimming level	Middle.
Feeding	Flakes, frozen and live foods.
Breeding	Can be bred in the aquarium, though rarely. Commercially bred in the Far East and Europe. Males are larger with tail fin extensions. Females are shorter and plumper with fewer colours. Egg-scatterer.
Special requirements	Groups, mature aquariums.

Notes – Emperor Tetras have a quality look about them that makes them popular subjects in planted aquariums. Males develop better colours and ornate tail fin extensions as they mature. A similar species is the Blue Emperor Tetra, *Impaichthys kerri*, which is bluer and doesn't develop the ornate fins.

Rummy Nose Tetra

Scientific name	*Hemigrammus bleheri*.
Origin	Rio Negro and Meta river basins, Brazil.
Size	4cm.
Tank size	60cm.
Tank type	Tropical community.
Water conditions	23–28°C, pH 6–7.5.
Ease of keeping	Moderate.
Swimming level	Middle.
Feeding	Flakes, frozen and live foods.
Breeding	Commercially bred in Europe and the Far East, though rarely bred in the aquarium. Males are smaller, with a brighter red head. Females are larger and plainer.
Special requirements	Groups, mature aquariums.

Notes – Rummy Nose look stunning when added in groups to planted aquariums, and the red head becomes even redder in soft acidic water. There are two other Rummy Nose species, but *H. bleheri* develops the reddest colouration.

Anabantoids

Anabantoids are special as they are air breathing fish. A special organ called the Labyrinth organ allows anabantoids to survive in poorly oxygenated water, by gulping atmospheric air from the water's surface they can survive in and exploit areas that other fish species cannot, giving them an advantage.

Opaline Gourami, Three-Spot Gourami

Scientific name	*Trichogaster trichopterus.*
Origin	Laos, Thailand, Cambodia and Vietnam.
Size	12cm.
Tank size	100cm.
Tank type	Tropical community.
Water conditions	24–28°C, pH 6–8.
Ease of keeping	Moderate.
Swimming level	Middle to top.
Feeding	Flakes, frozen and live foods.
Breeding	Can be bred in aquarium, though rarely is. Males build a bubble nest which the female lays eggs into. Males larger, more colourful with extended dorsal fin. Females shorter and plumper with a much shorter, stubbier dorsal fin.

Special requirements A spacious aquarium.

Notes – Blue Gourami are one of the few traditional tropical fish with blue colouration, and the striped blue form is known as the Opaline Gourami. Both are available in a gold form. They should be added to spacious tropical aquariums with other medium-sized fish. Males can be boisterous towards females, so keep two females to one male.

Siamese Fighting Fish

Scientific name	*Betta splendens.*
Origin	Thailand.
Size	5cm.
Tank size	30cm.
Tank type	Tropical community with small fish or single-species.
Water conditions	24–30°C, pH 6–8.
Ease of keeping	Moderate.
Swimming level	Top.
Feeding	Flake, frozen and live foods.
Breeding	Can be bred in the aquarium, with the female placing eggs into a bubble nest. Males are larger and more colourful. Ripe females are plumper.
Special requirements	Still water.

Notes – Siamese Fighters are well known, and well named, because of the vicious fight that ensues if two males are put together in the same tank. Sadly, they're more likely to be the victims of fin-nipping tank-mates these days, and are best kept as solitary specimens in a well-planted tank.

Honey Gourami

Scientific name	*Trichogaster chuna*.
Origin	India and Bangladesh.
Size	4cm.
Tank size	45cm.
Tank type	Tropical community of small fish.
Water conditions	22–28°C, pH 6–8.
Ease of keeping	Moderate.
Swimming level	Middle to top.
Feeding	Flakes, frozen and live foods.
Breeding	Can be bred in the aquarium, the female laying eggs in a floating bubble nest. Males are larger and more colourful, females are smaller and plain in colour.
Special requirements	Still or slow-moving water, a planted aquarium, and small peaceful tank-mates.

Notes – Honey Gourami look and behave in a similar way to Dwarf Gourami, only they're smaller and more delicate. Males become very colourful once settled, displaying orange, yellow and black colouration. Golden varieties are available and also one called Red Robin, though this should be avoided as its red colouration has been artificially enhanced with coloured foods.

Dwarf Gourami

Scientific name	*Colisa lalia*.
Origin	India, Pakistan and Bangladesh.
Size	7cm.
Tank size	60cm.
Tank type	Tropical community of small fish.
Water conditions	24–28°C, pH 6–8.
Ease of keeping	Moderate.
Swimming level	Middle to top.
Feeding	Flakes, frozen and live foods.
Breeding	Can be bred in the aquarium, with the female placing eggs into a floating bubble nest. Males are larger and more colourful, females are smaller, shorter in the body and less colourful.
Special requirements	Slow-moving or still water, a planted tank.

Notes – Dwarf Gourami are popular aquarium fish, though due to line-breeding to create more colour varieties they're not as hardy as they once were. Traditionally the female Dwarf Gourami was silver, but only coloured females are now available.

Pearl Gourami

Scientific name	*Trichogaster leerii*.
Origin	Sumatra, Borneo, Thailand and Indonesia.
Size	12cm.
Tank size	100cm.
Tank type	Tropical community.
Water conditions	24–28°C, pH 6–8.
Ease of keeping	Moderate.
Swimming level	Middle to top.
Feeding	Flakes, frozen and live foods.
Breeding	Can be bred in the aquarium, though rarely is. Males build a bubble nest and females lay their eggs inside it. Males are larger and more colourful, with a red breast and an extended dorsal fin. Females are plainer, shorter and plumper.

Special requirements A large tank with swimming space and planting.

Notes – Pearl Gourami are wonderful fish, though they're often overlooked these days in favour of more obviously coloured species. If left to mature in a large planted tank Pearl Gourami can become one of its key focal fish.

Freshwater invertebrates

Freshwater invertebrates are growing in popularity as more colourful species are being discovered, and they are exploited for their uses, like helping to rid an aquarium of algae for example. Freshwater invertebrates should only be mixed with small tropical fish as they are at risk of being eaten by any fish species that grows larger than 10cm in length.

Algae-Eating Shrimp

Scientific name	*Caridina multidentata*.
Origin	Japan, Korea and Taiwan.
Size	5cm.
Tank size	60cm.
Tank type	Community aquarium of small fish.
Water conditions	18–27°C, pH 6–7.
Ease of keeping	Moderate.
Swimming level	All levels.
Feeding	Dry foods, algae-based foods, algae.
Breeding	Can be bred in the aquarium, with the female releasing live young from her swimmerettes. Females are much larger and can be seen carrying eggs.
Special requirements	Small fish companions.

Notes – Algae-Eating Shrimp are popular because of the useful role that they play in planted aquariums. They're totally plant-safe, yet they clean every gravel grain and plant leaf in search for algae. They're often kept in CO_2-fertilised aquariums yet are sensitive to levels of CO_2 that are too high.

Crystal Red Shrimp, Red Bee Shrimp

Scientific name	*Caridina sp*.
Origin	Japan.
Size	2.5cm.
Tank size	30cm.
Tank type	Tropical community of tiny fish.
Water conditions	20–27°C, pH 6.5–7.2.
Ease of keeping	Moderate.
Swimming level	All levels.
Feeding	Dry foods, special shrimp foods, and algae.
Breeding	Can be bred in the aquarium. The females are larger and release live young from their swimmerettes. Females are larger and can be seen carrying eggs.
Special requirements	Only tiny fish as companions.

Notes – Crystal Red Shrimp are the red variant of the brown and white Bee Shrimp, and are highly prized amongst aquarists, so much so that they're graded according to the quality of their

red and white colouration and priced accordingly. Popular in planted tanks with CO_2 injection and nano tanks. Because they are so small, they should only be kept on their own, with other shrimps or tiny fish.

Cherry Shrimp

Scientific name	*Neocaridina heteropoda.*
Origin	Southern Asia.
Size	4cm.
Tank size	30cm.
Tank type	Tropical community of small fish.
Water conditions	18–30°C, pH 6.5–8.
Ease of keeping	Moderate.
Swimming level	All levels.
Feeding	Dry foods, special shrimp foods, and algae.
Breeding	Can be bred in the aquarium, and are usually prolific spawners. Females are larger and carry live young in their swimmerettes. Females can also be seen carrying eggs.
Special requirements	Only tiny fish as tank-mates.

Notes – Cherry Shrimp are less expensive than Crystal Red Shrimp and are prolific breeders once established in an aquarium. Popular in planted aquariums and nano aquariums, they're often added to aquariums fertilised with CO_2.

Assassin Snail

Scientific name	*Anentome helena.*
Origin	Unknown
Size	2cm.
Tank size	30cm.
Tank type	Tropical community of small fish.
Water conditions	23-27C, pH 6–8.
Ease of keeping	Easy.
Swimming level	Bottom.
Feeding	Other snails, sinking dry foods, algae.
Breeding	Livebearer? Sexual differences unknown. Can be bred in the aquarium.
Special requirements	Other snails for food.

Notes – Assassin snails are the perfect snails to introduce if you already have a problem with small nuisance snails. This is because they like nothing more than to eat other snails – which makes them an unusual but most welcome modern introduction to the community aquarium. Don't combine with any fish that eat snails, as they will themselves become prey.

Zebra Nerite Snail

Scientific name	*Vittina coromandeliana.*
Origin	Indo-Pacific region.
Size	Up to 25mm diameter.
Tank size	30cm.
Tank type	Tropical community.
Water conditions	20–26°C, pH 7–8.5.
Ease of keeping	Moderate.
Swimming level	Bottom.
Feeding	Dry foods, algae-based foods, algae.
Breeding	Unknown.
Special requirements	Algae, rocks.

Notes – The Zebra Snail and its relatives are highly desirable freshwater relatives of marine snails that are added to planted aquariums to help clear up algae, but not eat plants. Shell patterns are highly variable, making them collectable invertebrates, and they're much less invasive than most snail species. Shop specimens are often starving, so get them as soon as they come in. Always place them mantle down onto a rock so that they can fix their footing.

Brackish fish profiles

Bumblebee Goby

Scientific name	*Brachygobius xanthozonus.*
Origin	Java, Sumatra and Borneo.
Size	4cm.
Tank size	30cm.
Tank type	Brackish community of small fish, single-species.
Water conditions	25–30°C, ph 8.2, salinity 1.005–1.010.
Ease of keeping	Moderate.
Swimming level	Bottom.
Feeding	Tiny live and frozen foods, rarely accepts dry foods.
Breeding	Has been bred in the aquarium, though sexual differences are unknown. Egg-depositor.
Special requirements	Brackish water, small live foods.

Notes – Bumblebee Gobies are seen fairly frequently in aquatic shops though they're rarely given an aquarium that really suits them. They need a small quiet tank with lots of decor and hideaways and brackish water. Feed on cyclops, artemia, bloodworm and daphnia.

Mono

Scientific name	*Monodactylus argenteus.*
Origin	Indo-West Pacific region.
Size	27cm.
Tank size	180cm.
Tank type	Brackish community of large fish or full marine.
Water conditions	24–28°C, pH 8.2, salinity 1.005–1.024.
Ease of keeping	Moderate.
Swimming level	Middle.
Feeding	Flakes, frozen and live foods, marine foods.
Breeding	Has not been bred in the aquarium. Sexual differences unknown. Egg-scatterer.
Special requirements	Large aquarium, brackish water.

Notes – With their high bodies and extended fins Monos look like the marine version of Angelfish, *P. scalare*. Few people realise just how large they get and even fewer could accommodate a large shoal. Often displayed to effect in large public aquariums. Peaceful.

Scat

Scientific name	Scatophagus spp.
Origin	Indo-Pacific region.
Size	30cm.
Tank size	180cm and above.
Tank type	Brackish community of large fish.
Water conditions	20–28°C, pH 8.2, salinity 1.005–1.024.
Ease of keeping	Moderate.
Swimming level	All levels.
Feeding	Dry foods, frozen and live foods, vegetable matter and detritus.
Breeding	Have not been bred in the aquarium, sexual differences unknown. Egg-scatterer.
Special requirements	Large tank, varied diet, brackish water.

Notes – Scats are long-lived, large, high-bodied brackish fish that are gregarious feeders. Young specimens need to be fed frequently in order to maintain weight. Because of their large size they aren't often kept long-term, though some species have attractive juvenile colouration. Perfect accompaniment to Monos and Archer Fish.

Archer Fish

Scientific name	Toxotes jaculatrix.
Origin	Coastal regions from India to Northern Australia.
Size	Up to 30cm.
Tank size	180cm.
Tank type	Brackish community of large fish.
Water conditions	25–30°C, pH 8.2, salinity 1.005–1.024.
Ease of keeping	Moderate.
Swimming level	Top.
Feeding	Insects, frozen and live foods, carnivore sticks.
Breeding	Has not been bred in the aquarium. Sexual differences unknown. Egg-scatterer.
Special requirements	Brackish water, large aquariums, overhanging vegetation, insects.

Notes – The Archer Fish is world famous for its ability to shoot down insects from overhead branches. It does this by sending a jet of water from its mouth to knock down its prey. It even calculates for the angle of refraction by the water. It can also jump for prey nearer to the surface. Keep in groups in large brackish aquariums, ideally with overhanging decoration to encourage spitting.

Knight Goby

Scientific name	Stigmatogobius sadanundio.
Origin	India, Sri Lanka, Singapore and Indonesia.
Size	7.5cm.
Tank size	90cm.
Tank type	Brackish community of medium-sized fish.
Water conditions	22–26°C, pH 8.2, salinity 1.005–1.010.
Ease of keeping	Moderate.
Swimming level	Bottom.
Feeding	Frozen and live foods, some dry foods.
Breeding	Has not been bred in the aquarium. Males are larger with an elongated dorsal fin. Females are shorter and plumper.
Special requirements	Brackish water.

Notes – Knight Gobies are handsome fish that are often in a poor state when in the aquatic shop. Offer a well-decorated brackish tank with a sandy substrate and plenty of small meaty foods. Has been known to eat small fish, so beware.

Feeding

The proper feeding of your aquarium fish is paramount to keeping them healthy. A well-fed fish will be more likely to grow, develop better colours and even breed. A healthy fish will also be better equipped to fight off disease.

How to feed

To feed fish properly we must first look at their requirements. How do they feed in the wild? And what do they eat? Are they a carnivore eating meaty foods, or herbivore feeding on plant matter? How frequently do they eat, and does their diet change with the seasons? These are all questions that must be answered if your fish are to be provided with the best possible diet.

Predatory fish

Predatory fish and herbivorous fish are built differently, from the structure of their mouths and teeth to the length of their gut and intestines. Predatory fish are opportunistic feeders. They either let the prey come to them as they lie in wait, or they actively hunt prey down. Either way, they never know where their next meal is coming from, so they conserve energy as much as they can when they aren't hunting, and release a sudden burst of power to catch their prey when the opportunity arises.

Predators have expandable stomachs that can cope with infrequent, large meals. These fish can't always be choosy when it comes to prey size and many predators will tackle prey almost as large as themselves. Once they've gorged themselves on their meal they become sedate once more and can go days or even weeks without another large feed. Think of a predatory fish as being like a lion on the African savannah. They alternate between feast and famine, excess and lean periods.

Herbivorous fish

Herbivores are adapted to eat copious amounts of low-protein, high-fibre food. Typically eating detritus, algae and plant matter, their diets are relatively poor in nutrition, and to gain the nutrients that they need from their food they need to eat it constantly. Herbivorous fish have a long gut to process

Below: This predatory Tiger fish can tackle large prey, and is adapted to eat infrequently.

all of the plant matter that they consume, and they graze all day long. They move to find food, stay to graze that food source for as long as it's available, and then move on. Think of herbivorous fish as being like wildebeest on the African savannah, congregating in large numbers to avoid individual predation, and constantly on the move to find fresh grazing.

Omnivorous fish

The omnivores are much less specialised, feeding on most food sources as and when they become available. This gives them an evolutionary advantage over other fish, making it possible for them to eat both meat and plants. They aren't as good at eating meat as the predators, or as good at grazing plants as the herbivores, but they can eat both types and everything in between. Think of the omnivore's diet as being similar to our own. We can get by on all sorts of food, making us very successful at surviving in all sorts of habitat, but we do best of all on a diet that's varied.

Above: Yellow tangs are herbivores, grazing low protein foods all day long.

Below: This omnivorous Lake Malawi cichlid eats catfish eggs and parasites in good times, and algae growth when feeding is lean.

Predatory fish
Pike Cichlid
Piranha
Arowana
Stingray
Pictus Catfish

Herbivorous fish
Bristlenose Catfish
Molly
Tropheus Cichlid
Semaprochilodus

Omnivorous fish
Tiger Barb
Goldfish
Severum
Kribensis
Guppy

What to feed

In the aquarium we can't provide large expanses of aquatic plants for grazing, neither do we want to feed live fish to our predatory fish, so we feed them pre-prepared diets instead. Usually available in a dry form as flakes, these are fed to fish on a daily basis to provide them with all the vitamins, minerals and energy that they need. A standard tropical flake will be aimed at all fish, especially the omnivores, but if your fish have a more herbivorous or predatory diet then special recipes are available for them in dry form, as algae wafers for example for the herbivores, or carnivore sticks for the predators.

Dry foods in flake, stick, wafer, granule or tablet form are what we term staple foods for our fish, as, if they had to, they could survive, grow and breed from eating just these. Always feed your fish a staple dry food if you can, as they're also fortified with extra goodness, meaning that they provide lots of nutrition in a small package, even more than most natural foods that the fish would eat in the wild. This means that even the constant feeders can do very well on just two to three dry food feeds per day.

Above: Flakes are the most common aquarium fish food.

How often to feed

Once we've established whether the fish is omnivore, herbivore or predator, we can select the proper diet for them and also determine how often they should be fed. Remember that the predators eat large amounts infrequently in the wild, so this can be mirrored in the aquarium situation too. A large predator like an Oscar will only need to be fed ever other day with dry foods, and if feeding frozen foods

like shellfish or fish, they can eat so much of this rich food in one sitting that one or two feeds per week will suffice. In fact, overfeeding a predatory fish with protein-rich foods will make them fat, which will build to dangerous levels around their internal organs and shorten their lifespans. Don't give in to your clever predators if they beg for food every hour of

Below: Sinking tablet foods are great for bottom dwelling fish.

Below: Sinking algae wafers are specially made for algae eating fish.

every day. They may grow very quickly in the short-term, but it may shorten their lives in the long-term and put extra strain on your filter, as protein-rich foods convert into copious amounts of ammonia.

Since even herbivorous dry food diets are richer than what fish would obtain in the wild, two to three feeds per day is fine. If you're feeding tablets or algae wafers to your fish, each of these is a large amount of food for fish to digest in one sitting, and the intention is that the fish will graze on them for the rest of the day. To check whether you're giving them the right amount, drop enough wafers in to keep the grazers feeding on it for most of the day. If they're gone within an hour, give them more. If they're still on the bottom the next day, you're feeding them too many.

Omnivorous fish can be fed between one and three times per day on a standard tropical diet for all tropical fish. Feed them as much as they eat in about five minutes, and if there's any food on the bottom after ten minutes you're feeding them too much and should remove it with a net or gravel siphon to avoid it polluting the water. The best way to feed omnivores is little and often. Also, remember that small fish such as Neon Tetras have a faster metabolism than large fish, so should be fed more often regardless of dietary specifics.

Above: Feed your reef fish little and often with a variety of dry and frozen foods.

Frozen foods

These are supplementary foods that should be fed alongside a staple diet of dry foods. Frozen foods are usually made up of foods that were once alive, such as bloodworms, mosquito larvae, Brine Shrimp (also known by its scientific name of *Artemia*), cockles, Mysis Shrimp, Daphnia and Krill. These natural foods make up the diet of many freshwater and saltwater fish in the wild, and have the advantage of being recognisable by the fish as important food items that they should eat. They're also great conditioning foods. One interesting fact, however, is that although they're complete foods they contain very small amounts of nutrients, which on their own won't sustain a fish for very long.

To fortify frozen foods they can be soaked or sprayed in vitamin supplements, which is of great advantage to picky eaters such as seahorses that are very reluctant to eat dry foods.

How to feed frozen foods

Frozen foods come from aquatic stores either in blister packs or in bulk packs, and should always be stored in the freezer. Blister packs typically contain 24 foil-packed, sugar-lump-sized cubes of food, of which one or two are typically provided to a community of fish at each sitting. Bulk packs are slabs of food that can be broken into large pieces for

TIP

Feed algae wafers and tablets to your catfish after the lights have gone out at night. Most catfish prefer to eat in the dark, and omnivorous tank-mates will be less likely to steal their food.

feeding to larger fish, or to lots of tanks of fish in one go.

Frozen foods should be defrosted and rinsed first before feeding them to the fish. This isn't because the frozen food will harm the fish if they eat it frozen, it won't, as the cube would melt the second it hit the warm aquarium water anyway. The reason is that the ice that surrounds the frozen food is rich in phosphate and nitrogenous waste, neither of which are wanted in your aquarium water – phosphate can be a key algal trigger. To remove the ice, simply pop the cube out into a fish-catching net and rinse under the tap. Once defrosted, and with the waste from the ice washed away, the food can be placed into the aquarium.

Treat frozen fish food like you would your own frozen food. If a pack is accidentally defrosted, feed it to your fish there and then or throw it away. Do *not* refreeze it.

Live foods

Live foods are, as the name suggests, live, and are usually available from aquatic stores in the form of bloodworms, Brine Shrimp and Daphnia, though Tubifex worms and River Shrimp are sometimes available. Live foods have key advantages over frozen food, not only in that they're recognised by the fish as natural food, but also in the fact that their movements almost always stimulate a feeding response, even from the most difficult feeders.

Like frozen foods, live foods are natural and great for conditioning, but they're still quite low in nutritional values. Live foods such as Daphnia and Brine Shrimp can be enriched before being fed to the fish by feeding them algae-based liquid foods. The nutrition from the algae is then passed on to the fish when the live food is consumed. Feeding the live food will also prolong its life.

One problem with live food is that it's often pretty lifeless by the time you feed it to the fish. This is because it needs to feed constantly in order to stay alive and hold its nutritional value, and yet is usually packed in sealed polythene bags without any food. These bags quickly deplete in oxygen and become polluted, which kills the food inside.

To overcome this, either culture your own live food (you can buy Brine Shrimp hatching kits from aquatic shops) or

make sure that you buy the food as soon as it comes into the shop, while it's still fresh from the supplier. On hot days it can be kept alive for longer by putting it in the fridge.

How to feed live foods

As with frozen foods, the water that surrounds live foods in their little packages will be rich in waste, which you don't want making its way into the aquarium. Again, put the live food into a catching net first and rinse it vigorously under the tap before you feed it to the fish. Live food can also be sprayed with a vitamin supplement to provide extra nutrition.

Tubifex worms aren't often used as fish food these days because they naturally live in alluvial mud in river systems, and in the past few decades this has become polluted, which isn't good for fish. However, laboratory-grade Tubifex is available that will be free from pollution, and this can be fed to your fish in an interesting way. A cone worm feeder can be placed in the aquarium, from which the tiny worms

slowly make their way into the tank through the holes in the cone. Fish will go mad trying to eat the worms and will gorge themselves on them throughout the course of the day.

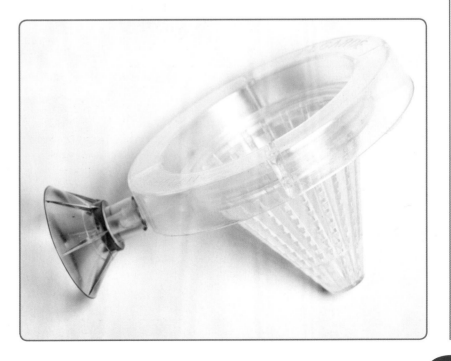

Maintenance

Maintenance is an essential part of keeping fish. Without it the water would become polluted with waste products; mulm and other debris would build up to dangerous levels; and algae would soon smother the glass. Filtration can only do so much, and every so often the water in the aquarium needs to be refreshed. Equipment may also need to be maintained in order to keep it running. Consequently without regular maintenance an aquarium soon becomes an inhospitable environment in which to keep fish.

Another reason to carry out maintenance is that it ensures your continued enjoyment of your hobby. This may sound strange, as maintenance is surely a chore, but without it you wouldn't be able to see your prized pets as the tank became smothered with algae. You wouldn't buy a new TV and let the screen get covered in so much dirt that you couldn't see anything, and the same applies to a fish tank. Algae is one of the biggest reasons why people give up the hobby. Keeping it at bay and keeping our aquariums looking great keeps us keen too.

Let's look at the different types of maintenance that need to be carried out, and how often it needs to be done.

Daily maintenance

■ Check that all the fish are present and correct, and that they're all healthy. This can be done easily when you feed them in the evening.
■ Check that the temperature is what it should be by using a thermometer.
■ Check that the filter is plugged in and running properly.
■ Check that the lights are coming on when they should. In very brightly lit tanks, wipe the front glass with an algae magnet to remove any build-up.
■ Feed the fish.
■ Add daily plant foods if necessary.

Weekly maintenance

■ Clean the inside walls of the aquarium with an algae pad or scraper.
■ Vacuum the substrate to remove debris, carrying out a small water-change at the same time.
■ Wash mechanical filter media in old tank water if necessary, or replace with new.
■ Test the four main water parameters – pH, ammonia, nitrite and nitrate – and if the nitrate levels are high, conduct a larger water-change. If ammonia or nitrite is present, investigate immediately.
■ Prune fast-growing plant species if necessary.
■ Add weekly plant foods if necessary.
■ Top up water to compensate for evaporation.

Left: An algae magnet is a quick and easy way to remove algae from inside the tank glass.

Below: Gravel vacuuming should be carried out on a weekly basis.

5 Essential tasks

1. Algae wiping.
2. Water changing.
3. Filter maintenance.
4. Water testing.
5. Fish feeding.

Monthly maintenance

- ■ Wash biological filter media in old tank water to remove debris.
- ■ Replace carbon if used.
- ■ Wipe down light tubes and/or cover glasses to remove any lime-scale or algae build-up.
- ■ Clean filter impeller and inlet/outlet pipes.

Yearly maintenance

- ■ Replace light tubes.
- ■ Check wear and tear on filter impeller and replace if necessary.
- ■ Buy new test kits to ensure that they remain in date.
- ■ Review the number and size of the fish in the tank, considering a larger tank if necessary.
- ■ Inspect the integrity of the cabinet and hood, considering replacement if necessary.
- ■ Buy new algae pad, scraper blade and algae magnet.
- ■ Consider a spring clean. Carry out a larger water-change than necessary, and re-aquascape to keep the tank looking good.

Right: Mechanical media should be rinsed in old tank water weekly, or replaced if necessary.

Below: Change water regularly, testing at the same time.

Combining maintenance tasks

The best way to conduct maintenance is to combine several jobs at once, which means less time is taken up with working, leaving more time for sitting back and enjoying. The best and quickest form of maintenance is to combine algae-wiping with substrate vacuuming, filter maintenance and water changing.

First wipe all the inside walls of the aquarium with an algae pad. Next vacuum the substrate, removing water as you do so and storing it in a bucket. Unplug the filter. Take the media out and wash it in old tank water. Discard the dirty water, put the filter back in, and replace the water with dechlorinated tap water. All of this can be done inside half an hour.

Some products can also aid maintenance, apart from the equipment listed on pages 120–121. Bacterial cultures can liquefy solid waste and improve water quality. Electrolytes and pH buffers can be added to maintain alkalinity, hardness and pH values and thereby avoid them crashing.

Maintenance equipment

Every fishkeeper should have these handy tools:

Gravel vacuum

Consisting of a siphon tube and wide-bore rigid pipe, gravel vacuums are simple but effective. The idea behind them is that the suction action of a siphon removing water from an aquarium can be harnessed inside a bigger tube to suck dirt from the gravel at the same time. By choosing the right-sized gravel vacuum you should be able to vacuum the whole aquarium base before removing all the water, providing a clean and a water-change at the same time. More elaborate vacuums are available, shaped to fit into corners, with grids to stop fish being sucked up, and with priming devices to save you from having to suck the pipe to get it started.

Algae magnet

A very handy piece of kit, this consists of two magnets of which one goes on the inside of the tank and one goes on the outside. They cling together, and where they meet they're covered in a soft polishing cloth on the outside surface of the glass and an abrasive pad on the inside surface. Slowly drag the outer magnet across the front of the aquarium and the inner magnet will follow it, removing algae as it goes.

Algae magnets can even go around the corners and clean the side panels of the aquarium. You get to clean your tank quickly, conveniently, and without even getting your hands wet.

They come in different shapes and sizes for different tanks. A small magnet will only be powerful enough to stick to and clean a small tank, so for a large tank you need a

large, powerful magnet. The most convenient form of algae magnet is the floating variety, so that if the inner magnet comes away from the glass it simply floats to the surface for easy retrieval.

Long-reach scraper

As its name suggests, a long-reach scraper is ideal for cleaning tall tanks and for cleaning algae from the back glass or acrylic. It's available with an abrasive pad, a plastic scraper or a metal blade, of which the last is the best option for removing stubborn diatom or calcareous algae deposits.

Algae pad

Perhaps the simplest cleaning aid of all, this is an abrasive pad designed to clean aquarium glass and remove algae. Only ever use aquarium-grade pads, as dishwashing pads may scratch the glass and contain cleaning agents that are poisonous to fish. If you're cleaning acrylic, a softer, acrylic-safe pad should be used.

Bucket

A bucket is essential when keeping fish, and has a number of uses. During maintenance, a bucket can be used to siphon water into, and to transport it to the drain and throw it away. It can also be used to wash mature filter media in tank water, and to replace clean water and top up.

Use a dedicated bucket or buckets just for fishkeeping, to ensure that no household detergents are used in them. The ideal bucket is one that has measurements on the inside, which can be used for dosing with dechlorinator, medications etc. The icing on the cake is a snap-top lid, which enables it to also be used to transport or hold fish.

Siphon tube

Any flexible piece of tubing can be used, though typically either a 12mm or 16mm diameter tube is used for removing water. A clear tube will enable you to see the water flow inside it, and what's flowing through it and into the bucket. Priming devices are available which connect to the end and save you from having to suck the pipe to get it started.

Motorised vacuum cleaner

These use a small, mains- or battery-powered pump to create the suction, and usually come with a gravel-cleaning attachment. Although no more powerful than a standard siphon-powered cleaner, battery-powered cleaners have the facility to trap waste in a fine net nag and return the water to the tank as they clean. This means that you don't have to do a water-change at the same time.

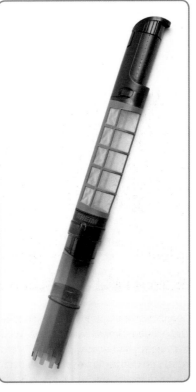

Fish health

Being able to identify and remedy problems with your fish is essential to keeping them alive. A basic knowledge of fish health is crucial.

Why do fish get ill?

As long as fish have been around on the planet, there has been a host of tiny organisms that prey on them, be they parasites, fungus or bacteria. In the aquarium it's no different, and as long as you keep fish it's highly likely that at some point you'll have to deal with the problem of some, if not all, of your fish becoming ill.

The main cause of fish disease is actually stress, as, like us, when fish are healthy they're normally able to fight off all sorts of ailments by themselves. It's only when they become run down that disease tends to affect them.

Stress is most commonly caused by poor water quality, so if your fish become ill you have to assume that they've become stressed prior to any symptoms appearing, and that a very likely cause will be poor water quality. Because of this connection between poor health and water quality, the first thing that you must always do is test the water. No matter how good the remedy, fish won't get better in poor water conditions, so water quality is the first thing that has to be fixed.

Disease diagnosis

Once you've established that the fish have become ill, you must ascertain what from, as different diseases have to be cured using different remedies.

Fish diseases can broadly be broken down into three categories – parasitic infections, bacterial infections, and fungal infections.

Parasitic infections

Whitespot

The most common parasitic infection that you're likely to encounter is called Whitespot or, to give it its scientific name, *Ichthyophthirius Multifiliis*, usually abbreviated to 'Ich' (or 'Ick').

Whitespot manifests itself as hundreds of tiny white spots all over the fish's body, usually starting on the fins. The white spots aren't actually the parasite itself, but rather a cyst formed on the skin as the parasite clings on. Whitespot is highly contagious and preys on fish that are stressed and overcrowded. If left untreated it could wipe out a whole tank, but if treated early enough it's usually easy to overcome with the right medication.

TREATING WHITESPOT

Although one stage of the parasite lives on the fishes' skin, fins and in the gills, Whitespot parasites have a lifecycle that involves reproducing in the substrate too. In severe cases remove all the substrate, thus removing a crucial life stage of the next generation of parasites.

Whitespot is also sensitive to high temperatures, and if your fish will tolerate it you should turn the water temperature right up to 30°C for a week or more. Finally, use

a Whitespot remedy as directed, which usually entails administering several doses over the course of a week.

Velvet

Velvet is often not seen at all until it's too late, or else is misdiagnosed as Whitespot. It affects fish in a similar way to Whitespot, and is just as contagious, only the spots are even smaller, more numerous and look more sticky and yellow (see photo above). Fish will also produce copious amounts of mucus to try to counteract the parasite. Velvet can quickly infect a whole tank of fish and could wipe them out if not treated quickly.

TREATING VELVET

Use an anti-parasite treatment, or one that's specific to treating slime and Velvet disease. It must be administered quickly and as directed on the bottle.

Argulus

Also known as Fish Louse, Argulus is a large crustacean parasite that can be seen with the naked eye. They grow up to 5mm in diameter and cling to fishes' bodies and fins and sometimes crawl inside the gills. Because they're so large they're resistant to many medications. If left they'll reproduce rapidly, and strings of eggs become visible on the substrate and on the glass. In severe infestations Argulus can even be seen swimming from fish to fish.

TREATING ARGULUS

Because of their size, Argulus can be physically removed from a fish using tweezers or your fingernails. Check inside the gills of large fish and then treat the whole tank with a treatment aimed at killing large crustacean parasites. Argulus is quite common on fancy goldfish, so inspect them carefully before you buy, and quarantine them in a bare tank to alert you of any warning signs.

Tips when treating fish

- Remove any carbon from the filter, as carbon soaks up remedies.
- Add extra aeration, as many diseases cause laboured breathing, and medications can strip oxygen from the water.

- Use a hospital tank for severe cases of illness, as medications work better in bare tanks. Copious amounts of decor and plants will soak up medication and make it less effective.
- Bright light breaks down medications, so turn the light off.
- Quarantine new fish in the first instance, making an outbreak of disease in the main tank much less likely. Quarantine tanks can double up as hospital tanks.

Bacterial infections

Bacterial infections are just as common as parasitic infections, and can even affect a fish as a secondary infection, after a parasitic attack. The bacteria are invisible, though fish affected by them will often show signs of white marks on the body or the tail, and will hang in the water or just below the surface looking very sorry for themselves. It takes a trained eye to spot early stages of parasitic infection, though clamped fins is normally a sure sign. Catch it early and things should be OK, but if it goes unnoticed it can wipe out most if not all of your fish, especially new arrivals. Some fish are more susceptible to bacterial infection than others, livebearing fish in particular. It's also more prevalent in overstocked, under-maintained aquariums.

Treating bacterial infections

First you need to ascertain that the infection is bacterial and not parasitic, so ask your aquatic expert at the shop. If you're

unsure you must add a broad-range medication that contains several chemicals known to knock out a variety of diseases. Once diagnosed, the best course of treatment is one that specifically targets bacterial infections.

Ask an aquatic expert if you are not sure if an infection is bacterial or parasitic. If unsure, use a broad-range medication.

Fungal infections

Fungal infections are quite easy to diagnose because of their cotton-wool-like appearance (see photo below). If a fish develops a fungal infection it's in real trouble, as these are

systemic, and can poison it. Fungal infections can also be the straw that breaks the camel's back if they come as a secondary infection after a parasitic disorder has resulted in the skin surface being broken by a fish flicking and rubbing to relieve irritation. Female goldfish are susceptible to fungal infection at spawning time as the skin thins on her flanks. Fungus must be treated as soon as it's spotted.

Treating fungal infections

Isolate the fish and use a treatment especially designed for fungus. As such infections normally result from physical injury to an individual, you rarely need to treat the whole tank. Improve cleanliness and hygiene in all tanks to stop the spread of fungal spores.

Other common diseases

Dropsy

This is another one that's quite easy to identify, though it's difficult to cure and almost always ends with the demise of the fish involved. Thought to be linked to bacterial infection, Dropsy occurs randomly in a community of fish and usually just affects one individual. The flow of water through the fish's body is put out of balance and the tissues swell up with water, making the fish look like a balloon. This in turn makes the scales stick out on end and the eyes pop out – a sure sign of Dropsy (see photo above).

There isn't much you can do to treat Dropsy and usually it's not indicative of any other problem in the main aquarium. Some treatments claim to be effective on Dropsy, but it's usually too late.

Fin Rot

A common problem on goldfish varieties, Fin Rot looks like white patches that start on the ends of the fins and from there can spread to the base of the fins and the body, eating away the fins as it goes and causing big problems for the fish (see photo below). Almost always caused by poor water quality in overstocked, under-filtered coldwater tanks, Fin Rot must be treated quickly using a medication aimed at treating both Fin Rot and fungus. If the rot is caught in time the fish will survive, though fin regrowth can take several months.

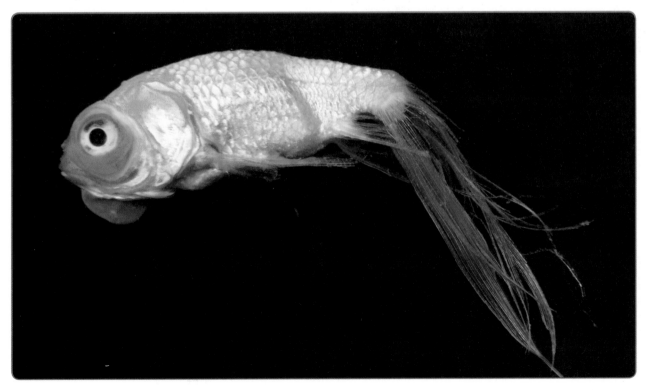

Breeding

One of the biggest bonuses with keeping tropical, coldwater or marine fish is that most have the potential to breed in an aquarium. Fish breeding can quickly grow from being an occasional accident to become an enthralling pastime. It could even earn you money.

Which fish breed?

Most fish will breed in the aquarium, providing that you supply them with a suitable mate of course; but some are far easier to breed than others. If you already keep fish you may have already bred them, as some species breed like proverbial rabbits. If you're new to the hobby, some of the most commonly recommended fish species are also some of the easiest to breed. Let's take a look at some commonly bred species and their breeding habits.

Livebearing fish

This interesting group contains popular species such as guppies, mollies and platies, and they're the easiest fish to breed of all, be they coldwater, tropical or marine. Livebearers are so-called because they give birth to live young.

Below: Livebearers, like this female guppy, breed readily in the home aquarium.

Male livebearers inseminate the females using an adapted anal fin called a gonopodium. The female's eggs are fertilised, and their bellies swell up as the fry hatch and grow inside them. About a month after being mated the female livebearer will give birth to 20 or more young, which are capable of swimming and feeding straight away.

Livebearers are great beginners' fish, and really easy to breed, so long as male and female fish are put together the females will become pregnant and give birth. In a heavily decorated aquarium with no predatory fish, livebearer young may survive to adulthood, with more and more fry coming all the time from their parents. They may even go on to produce offspring of their own. Guppies are so well known for their prolific breeding that one of their names is the Millions Fish. If left to their own devices livebearers can start a population explosion.

How to breed livebearing fish

CASE STUDY – GUPPIES

Taking guppies as an example, you'll need a male fish (usually with a large, colourful tail) and a female fish (usually larger than the male, but plain in colour). However, most livebearers will already be pregnant if they've been mixed with each other in the shop tanks. Pregnant female livebearers are known as gravid, and fat females often show a 'gravid spot', a black spot on the belly, which combined with their larger than average belly will indicate that they're pregnant.

If starting from scratch you'll actually need two or more females and one male, as males try to breed so persistently that the females can actually become quite stressed by it. Add more females than males, and the females can't all be chased at the same time. As soon as you mix the two sexes, the males will mate with the females.

As the females grow in size you'll need to make plans for separating them off to give birth. Lots of other fish will eat newborn livebearer fry, and interestingly the mother will also try to eat some as soon as they're born. To prevent this, the female should be placed in a tank on her own, with lots of feathery plants in which the newborn fry can hide to avoid predation.

Alternatively she can be placed in a special small tank called a breeding trap. This sits inside the main tank and has slots in the side to allow the circulation of water. The female is placed in the trap, over a grid, and when she gives birth the fry swim down through the grid into the lower portion of the trap where she can't get at them. As soon you spot the fry, remove the female, and for the first week or so the fry can be kept and fed inside the trap. Larger quarters will need to be found quickly, though, as the fry will need more room to grow than the trap can provide.

Breeding nets are also available, which provide a similar safe sanctuary for small fish in the main tank.

Feed the livebearer fry several times per day with liquid livebearer fry food, Cyclops, powdered flake and newly hatched Brine Shrimp. Within a few months they will reach adulthood and go on to breed themselves.

Egg-laying fish

Eggs are the most common method of reproduction in the fish world, and fish lay them in several ways. Egg-scatterers do as their name suggests, with the females scattering hundreds of tiny eggs over plants or the substrate. As the females scatter their eggs, the males scatter sperm and the eggs are fertilised. No parental care is provided and the adult fish may well go around eating their own scattered eggs after spawning. Well-known egg-scatterers include goldfish, danios, tetras, and barbs.

How to breed egg-scattering fish

CASE STUDY – DANIOS

To breed egg-scatterers such as danios, first make sure that you have male and female fish. Females are normally larger and fuller in the body. Males are usually smaller but with more colour. Buy a group of six if you're not sure, in the hope that you'll have both males and females amongst them.

Egg-scatterers don't breed all the time like livebearers do, and the fish need to mature and come into breeding condition first. At this time the females become plump with eggs. The males begin to drive the females around the tank,

Below: This Odessa barb breeds in typical egg-scatterer fashion.

showing off and nudging their vents. In a split second the females release a burst of eggs, and the males their sperm. The eggs then fall to the bottom.

To protect the eggs from their parents, a number of methods can be used. Marbles could be added to a bare tank, so that the eggs fall between them and are out of reach of the adults. Feathery-leaved plants could be used in abundance, in the hope that they'll catch the eggs in their leaves as they fall. Alternatively a synthetic, home-made 'plant' called a spawning mop can be used. This consists of a bunch of woollen strands used to catch eggs.

As soon as eggs are spotted, remove the fish from the tank and wait for the eggs to hatch into tiny fry within a few days. Very gentle filtration must be used so as not to suck up the newborn fry or the tiny first foods they require, such as liquid foods for the fry of egg-laying fish and newly hatched Brine Shrimp. Very tiny fry need even smaller foods, called infusoria.

Egg-depositors

Egg-depositors lay sticky eggs, and they lay them purposefully, in close proximity on a chosen site. That site could be on a piece of wood, a rock, a plant leaf or inside a cave. The most famous egg-depositors are cichlids, large, colourful, intelligent fish that actually protect and care for their eggs and fry. The

Below: Dwarf cichlids like this Apistogramma, deposit eggs and protect their young.

extra parental effort demonstrated by cichlids may mean that more of their young survive predation.

CASE STUDY – KRIBENSIS
Kribensis deposit their eggs in a cave, which the parents then defend from other egg- and fry-eating fish. You must start with a sexed pair, choosing a plump female with a red belly, and the larger, longer male with its spade-shaped tail.

As the female comes into condition she becomes fatter, more colourful and pays the male much more attention. When she's ready she'll lead him into the cave (made out of rocks, wood, a coconut shell or a flowerpot) and lay her eggs. At the same time he'll fertilise them. In a few days the eggs hatch into wrigglers, which stick inside the cave and later become free-swimming. This is the point at which cichlids come into their own, because the pair will then proceed to herd their small fry around the aquarium in search of food, frightening off other fish as they go. The fry should be fed on baby Brine Shrimp, Cyclops, powdered flake and liquid food for egg-laying fish.

Bubble-nesters

Bubble-nesters are egg-depositors of sorts, as males build a floating raft of bubbles at the surface of the water, and then the female lays the eggs underneath that. Often the male will protect the eggs and fry for a short time, and tend to the nest. Popular examples of bubble-nesters are gouramies and Siamese Fighting fish.

CASE STUDY – PARADISE FISH

First a sexed pair of Paradise Fish must be chosen. The male is larger, with longer fins and more colour than the female, which is also plumper. Males need something floating on the surface to which to attach their nest of bubbles; usually plant leaves will be fine.

The males spend several days blowing sticky bubbles at the surface until a raft of them has been created that's several inches across. He then displays to the female, enticing her over and eventually curling his body around hers in an embrace. She turns upside down, releasing eggs into the nest, and he fertilises them. In several days the fry hatch and hang around the surface. The male continues to protect them for a week or so, by which time the bubble-nest disperses. The fry must be fed on tiny live foods such as infusoria, and liquid foods for the fry of egg-laying fish.

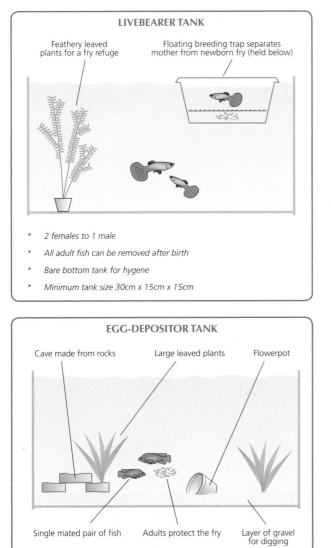

LIVEBEARER TANK

Feathery leaved plants for a fry refuge

Floating breeding trap separates mother from newborn fry (held below)

*   2 females to 1 male

*   All adult fish can be removed after birth

*   Bare bottom tank for hygene

*   Minimum tank size 30cm x 15cm x 15cm

EGG-SCATTERER TANK

Feathery leaved plants to catch eggs

Floating spawning mops made from wine corks and strands of wool to catch eggs

Layer of marbles to catch eggs

*   A group of mature male and female fish

*   3 methods of egg capture to ensure sucesss

*   Adults to be removed immediately after spawning

*   Minimum tank size 30cm x 15cm x 15cm

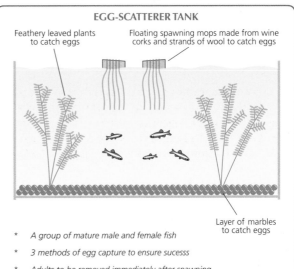

EGG-DEPOSITOR TANK

Cave made from rocks

Large leaved plants

Flowerpot

Single mated pair of fish

Adults protect the fry

Layer of gravel for digging

*   Leave parents with the fry

*   Minimum tank size 60cm x 30cm x 30cm

BUBBLE-NESTER TANK

Tall, feathery leaved plants that touch the water surface

Floating plants

Bare bottom tank

*   Single pair of mature fish

*   Remove female after spawning

*   Leave male with fry

*   Minimum tank size 60cm x 30cm x 30cm

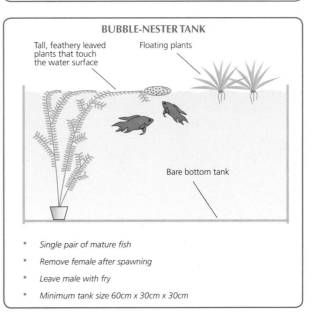

MARINE AQUARIUMS AND FISH

Marine aquariums

In terms of fulfilment, the marine side of the hobby has it all. Nothing can really compare to marines for shape and colour, and they have a following all of their own. As well as the fish there are also corals and invertebrates, which are certain to both impress and challenge you at the same time.

If you haven't ever kept fish before, then if you start with marines you should be warned that you're going in at the deep end. Marines are some of the most difficult to keep of all sea creatures, and it helps if you've had experience keeping coldwater or tropical fish first, in order to understand the basics of feeding, water testing and tank maintenance. Yet there are some benefits for the complete novice, since you'll otherwise need to largely disregard the basic principles of freshwater filtration and relearn it. Nevertheless, previous experience with keeping any sort of fish is invaluable.

The catch with keeping these exquisite fish and corals – and it's inevitable that there has to be a catch with something this beautiful – is that they demand exacting water parameters and are unforgiving of mistakes. The dream is to have a tank full of corals, shrimps, crabs and starfish, and the water above them teeming with fish such as you'd see on holiday or in a nature documentary. The reality, however, is that although this *can* be achieved, and while hobbyists are getting closer than ever to replicating natural

reefs, it takes time, money, understanding and determination, and if you haven't got these then maybe marines aren't for you.

This isn't intended to put you off too much, but merely to warn you. Since the majority of marine life is still taken directly from the oceans to grace our living rooms, we have a responsibility to offer it the best living conditions that we can at all times. The reefs in particular are a finite resource and are already fighting global warming, pollution, over-collection and damage by shipping. To counteract this we must act responsibly, researching livestock and its needs thoroughly before making a purchase, and educating even non-fishkeepers that corals are live animals and that we must do what we can to protect them.

The good news is that many marine hobbyists are doing just that, propagating their own corals and sharing them amongst friends who go on to build their own captive colonies and to spread the word about sustainability and the importance of understanding how natural reefs work. Even better, hobbyists are at the forefront of global coral propagation, and many people who started off keeping corals in their own living rooms are now offering advice to public aquariums and scientific organisations; and if it ever gets to the point where we start putting corals back into the ocean for reef revitalisation, we can take satisfaction from the fact that we've done a very good job learning about organisms that previously no one knew much about at all. It's only in recent decades that we even found out that corals were animals and not plants. What a long way we've come since then.

So as long as you act responsibly and treat the marine hobby not as a fad or a must-have fashion item, it can be incredibly fulfilling and diverse. To be at the point we've reached now, where we can create our own slice of living reef in the comfort of our homes, makes us very lucky indeed.

that floats by, and consistently clear, consistently pure saltwater that's low in nutrients. Imitate these conditions in a home aquarium and you should have no problem keeping marines. You could even make a smaller reef in a nano reef tank, though larger tanks are better because they're more stable and enable you to keep more fish.

What tropical marine life needs

Coral reefs only inhabit certain parts of the ocean, which provide them with what they need to survive. These include bright light from the full tropical sun, strong water movement from undercurrents, surge and waves, constant temperatures all year round, food from the planktonic life

Marine equipment

To create a reef environment at home you'll need the right equipment. Marine aquariums can vary in their equipment demands, depending on what you want to keep in them. Below are some typical equipment shopping lists, for different types of marine aquarium.

Nano reef with no fish

If you take fish out of the equation, a nano reef can be very small in volume, housing just shrimp, crabs, snails and coral polyps. They're great for desktops or strong shelves, and without having to feed any fish in there you can get away with not using a protein skimmer. The equipment listed below assumes that biological filtration will be taken care of by live rock.

- Tank.
- Powerhead (for flow, offering ten times volume turnover per hour).
- Heater (if placed in a cold room).
- Compact light (in marine spectrums and offering 1W per litre of water).
- Test kit .
- Hydrometer (for measuring salt content).
- Thermometer.

Nano reef with fish

When you include fish in a nano tank you must provide them with enough space to exercise, and a volume of water that's stable enough to cope with their waste products. A volume of 45 litres or more is recommended for keeping fish, as well as some form of nutrient removal such as a skimmer. The equipment listed assumes that live rock will be used as the main form of filtration. The list can be scaled up to any size of tank containing soft corals, and is the basis of the Berlin system (see page 137).

- Tank.
- Powerhead(s).
- Heater.
- Compact light.
- Test kit.
- Hydrometer.
- Thermometer.
- Protein skimmer.
- UV (optional, but useful for controlling marine Whitespot on surgeonfish).
- External filter (optional for packing with chemical media, such as phosphate removal media or carbon). Remove all biological media, as filtration will be done by live rock.

Above: Chillers are useful, but optional pieces of equipment.

Above: Calcium reactors aid coral growth

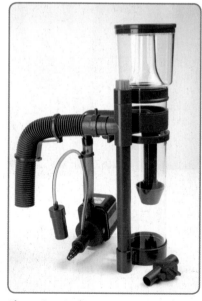

Above: Protein skimmers are essential for any marine aquarium containing fish.

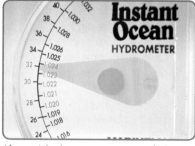

Above: A hydrometer measures salinity.

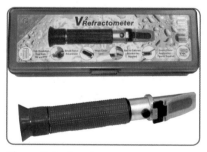

Above: Refractometers are very accurate.

High-tech reef aquarium for stony corals

This is the state-of-the-art in reef-keeping, where aquarists attempt to successfully keep the reef-building corals that typify a natural coral reef. Lighting is brightest at the reef crest, and water movement is at its strongest. These corals are the least tolerant of high temperatures, high nutrient levels, low lighting and low levels of flow. Because high-powered lighting produces a lot of heat, a heater is rarely necessary.

As you can see, the list of equipment is seemingly endless, and calcium reactors, chillers, top-up systems and computers aren't cheap to buy, or to run. Every piece of equipment will also need to be plugged in, which makes plumbing and wiring such a system quite an engineering project in itself. Get it right and the results will be spectacular. Get it wrong and it will be one equipment nightmare after another. It's only recommended that experienced aquarists take on a project such as this, and even they will need to be sure that they have the financial resources, the time and the technical skill to keep it going.

- Tank (drilled tank is optional).
- Large flow pumps (delivering 20 times water circulation per hour or more).
- Wavemaker (optional device for alternating flow patterns).
- High-powered metal halide lighting (delivering 1W per litre of water or more).
- Test kits (pH, ammonia, nitrite, nitrate, phosphate, calcium, alkalinity, magnesium).
- Refractometer (more accurate at reading salinity than a hydrometer).
- Thermometer.
- Protein skimmer.
- UV (optional).
- Sump (optional, but recommended to hold all the equipment).
- Refugium (either hanging on the back of the main tank, or fitted within the sump).
- Calcium reactor (to supply calcium and magnesium to growing corals).
- CO_2 system (to supply calcium reactor).
- Chiller (essential to control the temperature in systems with high levels of lighting).

Above: Nano reef aquariums are very popular.

- Computer (optional monitoring equipment that can also control flow patterns and lighting and read salinity etc).
- Phosphate reactor (optional piece of equipment to draw as much phosphate out of the system as possible, to provide the best possible conditions for stony corals).
- Automatic top-up system (optional, but useful for systems with high daily evaporation).
- Reverse osmosis unit (optional, for topping up evaporation and making up salt water for water-changes).

Below: A stunning high-tech reef for stony corals.

Marine filtration

If you kept freshwater fish before and understand the biological processes, be warned that they're a bit different for marines. If you're going straight into marines, the learning curve can be steep, but once it sinks in its easy.

Biological filtration

As we know from freshwater filtration, biological filtering is the most important part of maintaining good water quality. In marine aquariums you could use the same ceramics and sponge materials for harbouring bacteria, but it's best not to.

As we know, ammonia is converted by bacteria to nitrite and then nitrate, only we don't want any of these pollutants in marine aquariums, especially with very sensitive livestock. When you biologically filter a marine aquarium you actually use a rather nice form of decor called live rock, which acts like huge lumps of ceramic biological media, providing a home for beneficial bacteria in the main tank. So, use live rock and you'll get both decor and filtering; use conventional freshwater methods and you'll just end up with lots of nitrate.

Biological filtering also works slightly differently in marine aquariums, as such is the diversity of the organisms that they can also consume nitrate (another advantage of live rock versus normal media) in a much more complete nitrification process. The ideal is to have ammonia broken down and converted by aerobic bacteria on the outer surface of the rock, and then to have the resultant nitrate broken down by anaerobic bacteria both within the rock and within the fine grains of sand at the bottom of the aquarium.

But you can also try to bypass biological filtering and waste reduction altogether, or at least give it a helping hand…

Protein skimmers

Protein skimmers are a type of mechanical filter that only really works in saltwater. They work by creating very tiny bubbles that rise up inside a tube, collecting proteins as they go. When they get to the top of the tube they become a foam, which overflows into a collection cup. The residue from the foam collects, and is then thrown away.

Proteins contain ammonia, so an effective protein skimmer can also remove ammonia before it breaks down into nitrite

Left: Live rock is used for biological filtration.

Above: A hang-on protein skimmer.

Right: A sump based protein skimmer.

What makes a good protein skimmer?

To remove proteins effectively, the foam needs to have a large surface area consisting of lots of tiny bubbles rather than a few large ones, and good contact time, meaning that the bubbles are in contact with the aquarium water for as long as possible before they overflow into the collection cup. The skimmate produced in the cup should be dirty, grey/brown and smelly, and have the consistency of gravy. This proves that lots of waste is being removed from the water, and is known as a 'dry skim'. A wet, yellow skimmate is known as a 'wet skim', and may mean that the skimmer needs to be adjusted.

Right: Good water circulation is vital with Berlin systems.

Below: Fine bubbles rise and collect protein.

Bottom: A good skimmate will be brown and smelly.

and nitrate, neither of which are wanted in seawater. This pre-filtering and mechanical removal lessens the burden on live rock and helps to maintain a much cleaner aquarium, which is important since corals and invertebrates need very clean water that's low in nutrients in order to survive.

The Berlin system

Protein skimmers can be combined with live rock to provide both mechanical and biological filtering in the main aquarium, and the two combined can be very effective. A marine reef aquarium filtered just by live rock and a protein skimmer is called a Berlin system, the invention of which several decades ago revolutionised the marine hobby and made it possible for us to keep so many of the creatures that we keep today.

There's another key factor to the Berlin system, however, and that's one of flow. To keep aerobic bacteria alive on the rock, and provide them with their food and essential oxygen from the water column, we must provide water movement.

Traditionally this can easily be done by pointing powerheads at live rock, and adding enough powerheads to provide a combined aquarium volume turnover of ten times per hour. This has the added advantage of providing sufficient water movement for soft coral species, and the improved water quality and water movement that the Berlin system provides proved to be a cornerstone in the development of the hobby.

Modern Berlin systems allow for the growth of much more difficult stony corals, with even better skimming and higher flow turnover of 20 times volume per hour or more.

Right: Sump based skimmers fit neatly inside the cabinet.

TIP

Choose a protein skimmer model that can deal with up to twice the volume of your aquarium. When relying on a skimmer as a key element in your filtration, don't skimp – choose a model that offers the best possible performance.

Sumps

Sumps are aquariums that sit underneath the main aquarium and harbour equipment and/or filter media. They can be used for fresh or saltwater systems, though they really come into their own with marines.

Marine aquariums typically utilise lots of different pieces of equipment, all doing different jobs, and this can clutter the main aquarium and make it look unsightly. Not all protein skimmers will fit directly to the main aquarium either, as they won't stretch over stress bars and need a lot of clearance above the waterline. A sump can house the protein skimmer, heater, circulation pump and pipework for a UV, chiller and calcium reactor. It could even house live rock, live sand and macro algae in a special sump tank called a refugium.

When considering a sump you must also consider the main tank above it. Overflow kits are available that take water from the tank above to the sump below, but the best type of tank to feed water to the sump is one that contains a weir. This is a box built into the main display tank, behind which is a hole. The weir prevents the whole tank's contents from pouring down the hole; instead only the excess water flows over the top of the weir (which is at the top of the tank). A pump sits in the sump below and pumps water into the main tank. It's circulated around the tank before overflowing the weir and falling back into the sump, taking debris and waste water with it. While in the sump, the water is heated, filtered, skimmed and then returned and recirculated in the main tank.

Other advantages

A bit like an external filter, a sump has the advantage that any maintenance you do to it leaves the main tank, and the fish above, undisturbed. Because it's open-topped and not a sealed canister, water-changes can also be carried out in the sump below, as too can the topping up of evaporation.

Marine tanks are notorious for high levels of evaporation – sometimes 2–3cm every few days – and without a sump

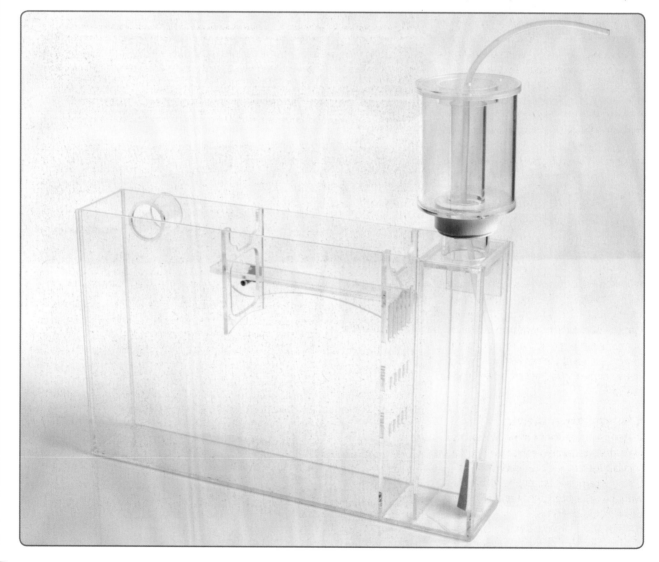

this means that the water level will visibly drop in the main tank. High evaporation can expose corals, as can conventional water-changes, but a sump combined with a weir in the main tank will maintain water levels in the top tank, and you just top up the sump below.

Sumps can also increase water volume.

Refugiums

A very popular filtration method, or main system add-on, is a type of sump called a refugium. All reef aquariums produce microscopic live foods, which are grazed – or perhaps over-grazed – by the reef-inhabiting fish in the tank above. But microscopic creatures have benefits for the whole system. Some are detritivores (meaning they consume solid waste on the aquarium floor), and when they reproduce their offspring feed corals.

Beneficial algae can also be kept in a refugium with a light, where they can grow and consume nutrients such as nitrate and phosphate without being eaten by herbivorous fish such as tangs and dwarf angels.

But one of the best features about a refugium is that by providing a safe home for creatures it causes their numbers to rocket, and the overpopulation simply falls into the pump chamber from where it's pumped into the main tank, providing perfect live food for fish and corals alike. Macro algae can be harvested and fed to fish too.

Choosing a sump

If you're unsure about the whole sump/weir idea, get expert advice from a marine specialist store. They can pick you the correct sump, design and build a tank with a weir, and ensure that there won't be any leaks or floods.

Sumps can even be bought off-the-shelf in specialist stores, complete with

main tank volume and pump recommendations. When the power goes off, a small amount of water from the main tank will trickle back down the pipework and into the sump, and the sump needs to be large enough not to overflow when that happens – typically 60 x 30 x 30cm and above.

Marine lighting

As mentioned on pages 26–9, marine lighting must be sufficiently bright for the organisms that use it, and of the right spectrum.

Why do corals need light?

Well not all corals do, but the colourful ones that we like to put in our reef aquarium do, and that's because they harbour something quite special within them.

Corals feed in two ways, by catching zooplankton with their polyps – which in some species only come out at night – and through special, symbiotic algae called Zooxanthellae that live within their tissue. Zooxanthellae work like plants,

TIP

When choosing the lighting that's best for you and corals, first make sure that it will fit on to your chosen tank. Metal halides need open-top tanks, and open air so that they don't overheat. If you're using lots of fluorescent light tubes, have you left yourself room inside the hood for routine maintenance?

photosynthesising in the daytime and providing the coral with extra energy. Without bright light the algae can't photosynthesise and may die off, and without algae the coral loses half of its food supply, which endangers its other life processes.

So a reef aquarium is a harmony of biological processes,

Above: Mushroom corals only require low light.
Right: Small polyp stony (SPS) corals require high light.
Opposite: Bright metal halide light illuminates this stony coral reef.

all working together to provide the vibrant scenes that we see in nature. Bacteria are breaking down fish waste, light is feeding corals and growing phytoplankton, phytoplankton is being fed on by corals and zooplankton, and zooplankton is being fed on by corals and fish. Corals provide protection and food for reef fish, and so the cycle goes on.

Duration, brightness and spectrum

For reef-building corals to do well they need bright light that replicates sunlight. As mentioned earlier, marine water filters out the red, yellow and orange parts of full-spectrum sunshine, leaving mostly white and blue light, which the corals are adapted to use. We can provide that light to them by either using fluorescent, metal halide or LED lighting.

Depending on where they live on the reef, and at what depth, different species are adapted to different levels of light. The list below will give you an idea of what coral types need in terms of lighting, and what that equates to in terms of lighting equipment in a reef aquarium.

- Low light = 4 x T8 or 2 x T5 with reflectors – some hardy soft corals such as Mushrooms, Finger Corals and Toadstool Corals if the aquarium isn't too deep.
- Medium light = 4 x T5 with reflectors – all soft corals, Mushrooms and most large polyp stony corals such as Bubble Coral.
- High light = Metal halide lighting + T5 actinic – some soft corals, some large polyp stony corals, all small polyp stony corals such as Acropora.

Things to think about with lighting

- All lighting can penetrate further, and be up to 100 per cent more efficient when fitted with reflectors. Without them 50 per cent of the light source will be shining up away from the aquarium.
- It's best not to use any cover glasses with bright lighting, as splashes, algae growth and salt creep will seriously degrade the lighting travelling through the glass. Do without them and use splash-proof lighting instead.
- Metal halide bulbs can degrade in spectrum and quality of light in as little as six months. Change them regularly to keep the quality of light to your light-loving corals as it should be.
- Always leave lights to cool for at least half an hour before touching and replacing them. Bright lighting can scald.
- Never touch metal halide bulbs with your fingers – wear latex gloves or cradle the bulb in tissue. The oils on your fingers will mark the bulb.
- Plug lighting into a timer so that it comes on at the same time every day and your livestock can adapt to a cycle of night and day. Plug actinic blue lighting into a separate timer that comes on before the main lights, and goes off after the main lights, providing dusk and dawn effects, and gradually acclimatising your fish and invertebrates to the bright light.
- Don't have lighting on for more than 12 hours per day. Any more is more than a natural reef would receive, and will cause excess heat and nuisance algae growth.

Marine flow

It's said by some experts that although many corals can survive with light, none can survive without water flow. Providing adequate water movement in a marine aquarium is paramount to its success.

To see just how much the sea moves around, you don't need to travel all the way to a coral reef. Any coastline in any part of the world will dramatically illustrate the power of the ocean's tides and currents, and how those currents have shaped the way that all marine life lives.

Unlike a river, whose flow is laminar and unidirectional, a marine environment is subject to times of surge, ebb and flow, alternating direction, storms and tides. The water never stops moving in the ocean, and flow can be particularly strong around reefs as currents originating in deep, open water are forced up into shallow water, and crash against the reef structure. Corals are known as sessile invertebrates, and on the whole once they're attached to a rock structure they can't move to a better position, unless they grow and spread to it, and that's a pretty slow process.

Yet corals are animals that need to feed, and produce waste. Water movement around them brings food in the form of planktonic life, known as zooplankton, but it also washes away their waste products, which is essential if they aren't to poison themselves with their own waste. Without strong water movement, corals die.

Creating flow in the aquarium

Luckily, moving water in an aquarium is quite easy, and we borrow the simple technology from power filters and pond pumps to create pumps and powerheads that move water by way of an impeller.

For many years powerheads were the best way to move water around, as they were readily available, relatively inexpensive and could be used on their own in the tank, as

they also came with inlet strainers to prevent fish and shrimp from being sucked in and killed. An average 100-litre marine aquarium could be fitted with two 500lph (litres per hour) powerheads or one 1,000lph powerhead, and its ten-times volume flow requirements would be taken care of without much fuss.

Two powerheads can even be plugged into a wave-making device, which alternated power supply from one to the other, creating a push and pull effect in the water and simulating natural flow patterns. This method can still be used today and is part of the backbone of the very successful Berlin system, in which pumps blow water across living rock and the rock breaks down the waste. The same pumps also supply food items to corals as they flow past, and wash away their waste.

Modern flow pumps

As we required more and more flow, for larger tanks and more demanding stony coral species, the number of powerheads needed in a tank began to build up to the point where they became unsightly, produced heat and consumed lots of electricity. They also provided high velocity flow in a small area, meaning that they were too powerful for a coral when close up, but too weak when placed further away.

The solution was to totally redesign powerheads, creating a new type of pump that could turn over large water volumes, across a larger area, but at slower velocity and using less energy. The modern flow pump was born.

With modern flow pumps, much higher tank volume turnovers can be achieved, of say 20–50 times tank volume per hour, but using less pumps and less heat and energy. Flow pumps are the best choice for a reef aquarium, and are also available in low voltage forms and types that can be controlled by sophisticated wave-making devices. Modern wave-makers can control four large pumps at once, and produce several pre-set flow patterns for a very natural simulation. They can even lessen the flow at night, and sense when the lighting is off.

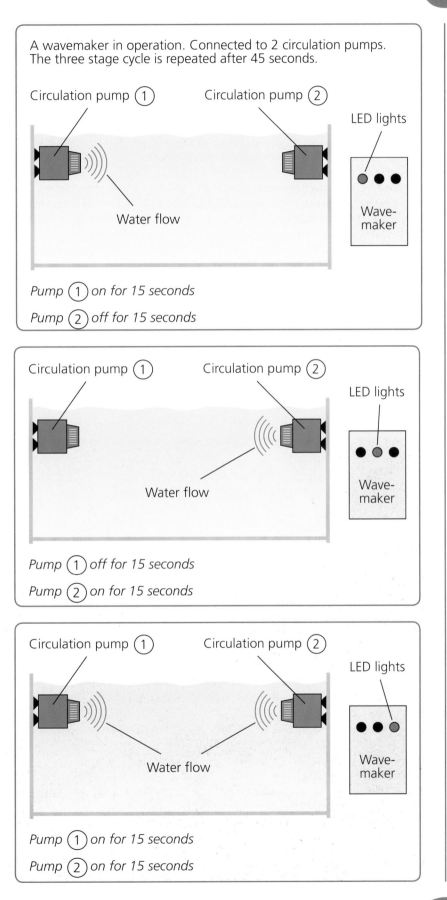

A wavemaker in operation. Connected to 2 circulation pumps. The three stage cycle is repeated after 45 seconds.

Circulation pump ①   Circulation pump ②   LED lights

Water flow   Wave-maker

Pump ① on for 15 seconds
Pump ② off for 15 seconds

Circulation pump ①   Circulation pump ②   LED lights

Water flow   Wave-maker

Pump ① off for 15 seconds
Pump ② on for 15 seconds

Circulation pump ①   Circulation pump ②   LED lights

Water flow   Wave-maker

Pump ① on for 15 seconds
Pump ② on for 15 seconds

Marine temperature

Contrary to what you might think, the biggest problem with tropical marine aquariums is not keeping them warm, but keeping them cool. Although situated on the periphery of hot countries, coral reefs have quite a constant all-round temperature. If temperatures change they change very slowly, and if they ever rise much above 27°C the coral reef's inhabitants can be in real trouble.

Hot temperatures

Hot temperatures cause many problems for reef inhabitants, but mainly for corals and invertebrates. If stressed by heat, photosynthetic corals and anemones can go through something known as bleaching, where all the symbiotic Zooxanthellae algae is shed. This leaves the organism without a major source of food and is a sure sign that something has gone badly wrong in the aquarium. Too much heat in the ocean causes bleaching too, and reefs in the wild are today threatened by rising sea temperatures.

Causes of heat in the aquarium

The most obvious heat source in a marine aquarium is the heater/thermostat itself, though most hobbyists remove the heater after setting up, as they realise that the lights are providing more than enough heat.

A word of warning about heaters – low-quality heaters may fail in the 'on' position, boiling your fish and corals. With the average reef aquarium containing hundreds if not thousands of pounds' worth of livestock, is it really worth risking it all by buying a low-quality heater? If you need to heat your aquarium, buy the best heater that you can get hold of.

The next biggest source of heat in an aquarium is the lighting. Metal halides and copious amounts of T5 lighting

Below: Cool running LED light will help to prevent overheating.

Above: A chiller is essential in prolonged heat waves.

Above: Fan cooling can be cheap and effective.

produce a lot of heat – enough to heat a room, let alone an aquarium – and water takes longer to cool down than air does. It's quite likely that if you have a home aquarium with four T5 lights or metal halide lighting you'll notice via your thermometer that the water temperature rises above that set by the heater on a daily basis. The more enclosed the lighting is, the worse the problem becomes, as the heat can't escape. Lighting ballasts produce a lot of heat too.

There's one item of equipment that you wouldn't expect to produce heat, and that's the pump. But flow pumps and powerheads produce heat, and generally speaking the more powerful they are, and the more electricity they consume, the more heat they'll produce; and they're on 24 hours per day, all year round. Think also of your skimmer pump, your sump return pump, and the pumps on calcium reactors and phosphate reactors. They all consume electricity and add to the heat in the aquarium.

Finally there's the threat of external conditions such as summer heat waves. Reef aquariums only require a temperature of 25°C, yet frequent summer heat waves could send the temperature to 30°C or more. If this happens you must take immediate action.

Cooling down your aquarium

Quick fixes

The best way to cool an aquarium is by installing an aquarium chiller. Popular in hot countries, they work like a refrigerator, using a coolant to cool the water and venting off all the heat. Advantages include adjustable temperature control, usually to half a degree Celsius; so you could set a chiller to come on at 24.5°C and, if correctly rated to the size of the tank, it will make sure that the temperature never exceeds that figure. Some chillers can heat too, ensuring perfect, constant temperature.

The downside with chillers is that they're expensive to buy and expensive to run, as they use a lot of electricity. They need to have water fed to them by a pump or external filter, and if placed in the same room as the aquarium the heat that they vent off into the room in turn heats the tank, causing a vicious cycle as the chiller comes on more and more often, and more and more heat is vented into the room. For chillers to work properly they should be placed in a well-ventilated area, away from the main tank. Even so, if you have an expensive marine collection chillers save lives, despite their faults.

Fans

Any fan will do, from small computer fans to large desk fans. Simply by blowing cool air across the surface of the aquarium, a fan will help to keep it cool. If you're using small computer fans inside a hood, turn one inward to blow cool air into the hood, and one at the other end outwards, to suck hot air out of the hood.

Long-term solutions

If heat and the cost of cooling is a long-term problem, evaluate all the equipment that's fitted on the tank. If using hot metal halide lighting, could you have it on for a few hours less every day, or replace it with cool-running LED lighting? Could you replace two pumps with one larger but more efficient one? And does your calcium reactor need to be on all day?

Cutting down on electricity and heat will not just help you out, but will help the planet too, as less energy used means a greener hobby.

Marine salt

The most fundamental difference between freshwater and marine is, of course, the presence of salt. But you can't use just any salt, especially not table salt, as it's quite different to what comes out of the sea.

Salt water is actually a soup of all known elements, containing large quantities of some and small quantities of others. It's much more than just sodium chloride and water. Some elements such as calcium, magnesium, chlorine, strontium, potassium, boron, fluorine and sulphur, are present in fairly high concentrations, but others – the 'trace elements' – are found in much lower levels.

To keep our marine livestock healthy we either use salt taken from the sea and refined during a desalination process, or, for the most part, we buy synthetic salt mixes that have been developed in laboratories to mimic the marine environment perfectly. Salts used to be formulated to be used in conjunction with tap water, which contained its own levels of elements and hardness, but since most marine keepers use purified RO water these days the formulation selected will need to contain increased elements in order to compensate for this.

Why use RO water?

Reverse osmosis is recommended as the base for making up saltwater because it's had everything removed from it, enabling you to make perfect saltwater from scratch. Using tap water is more convenient and cheaper, but the nitrates and phosphates that it contains can harm invertebrates and retard the growth of corals.

Deionised water can also be used, and is said to be even better than RO because a deioniser can also remove the silicates – another algal trigger – from tap water. However, DI water is more expensive to produce than RO, so some units combine an RO as a pre-filter, and then connect to a DI for final polishing. This prolongs the lifespan of the DI media, as the RO has already taken most of the nasties out by the time the water gets to it.

Which salt should you choose?

As long as you buy a specially prepared aquarium marine salt from an aquatic store, and mix it to the right concentration, there's no right or wrong salt to buy, and all will achieve the desired results. With the focus being more on reef aquariums these days, many brands will advertise that they don't contain nitrate or phosphates, which is good, and that they'll guarantee high levels of calcium and magnesium, which are essential for coral growth.

Salt can be expensive, but is necessary, and you'll always need some lying around in case you have to do an emergency water-change. You can save money in the long-term by buying in bulk, and a 25kg bucket of salt will work out much cheaper in the long-term than buying small 2kg bags or boxes.

Left: Modern salts are designed to be used with RO water.

Below: Hydrometers often show 'safe' salinity levels.

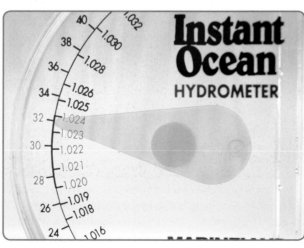

Mixing saltwater

Surprisingly this is one of the aspects of keeping marines that puts many people off, but it's straightforward and easy to do, and when you've done it once and noticed that all your marine life is still OK you'll be much more confident about doing it again.

1 Get a clean bucket of RO water, and bring it to temperature with a heater. Use a thermometer to measure the temperature. It will be ready when the temperature reaches 25°C. Temperature is crucial when mixing salt, as hydrometers and refractometers are calibrated to read salt levels at a specific temperature, which is usually 25°C.

2 Add cupfuls of salt to the RO water. A neat way of estimating how much to put in is actually to weigh it. A salinity of 1.024 equates to 35g of salt per litre of water, so for a 10-litre bucket of RO water you'll need to add 350g of salt.

3 Dissolve the salt thoroughly into the water, first of all by stirring the large piles with your hand, and then by adding a powerhead or airstone to the bucket. Put the heater back in and leave until the salt has properly dissolved. The best way is to make up salt water the day before you need it, and leave it to thoroughly mix overnight.

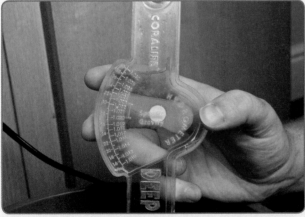

4 Use a hydrometer or refractometer to accurately measure the salinity, or specific gravity (sg), of the water. Aim for a level of 1.024. If it's too salty, add some pure RO. If it's not salty enough, add more salt.

5 Pour the water into the tank.

Other marine equipment

Ready to set up a marine aquarium? Here's a shopping list of essentials and useful items:

Essential

- Hydrometer – essential for measuring how salty the water is. For a more accurate measurement use a refractometer.
- Test kit – essential for monitoring water quality in the main aquarium. As well as the main four tests, also consider test kits for phosphate, calcium, magnesium and alkalinity.
- Phosphate remover – essential for removing phosphate, which in turn causes nuisance algae and retards the growth of corals and calcareous algae.

- Salt – essential for all marine aquariums. Only use salt intended specifically for the production of water for marine aquariums.
- RO water – essential for providing nitrate- and phosphate-free base water in which to mix the salt. Tap water may be OK for marine-fish-only aquariums but it's no good for reef aquariums.
- Bucket – essential for mixing saltwater, removing water from the aquarium and acclimatising fish and corals. Always use a specific bucket just for your marine aquarium, and never use it for any other jobs such as domestic cleaning.
- Siphon tube – essential for removing water from the aquarium. It can also be connected to a gravel vacuum, and used to clean the substrate while it remains in situ.
- Algae scraper – essential for removing algae in a marine aquarium, which proliferates even more quickly than in freshwater because of the greater light and high pH and alkalinity. For tough calcareous algae, use a scraper with an aluminium blade; for daily wiping of the front glass a strong algae magnet will suffice.

Useful

- Towels – the marine hobby can be a messy one, especially as splashes of saltwater contain salt, and drips will be more visible. Use old towels when conducting maintenance, both to protect the floor and to wipe up any spills.
- Carbon – a useful chemical media to be used in the short-term. Place high-grade carbon into the filter or loose in a

net bag and it will soak up some organics, dyes in the water and odours. Don't use it all the time, though, as it can remove useful supplements from the water too. Clearer water means better light penetration for corals.

■ Jug – you never know when you're gong to need a jug, but you're likely to need one quite often. Jugs are useful for topping up evaporation, and for mixing supplements. Use a measuring jug for accurate dosing.

Optional

■ Calcium reactor – A complicated piece of kit that uses carbon dioxide to lower pH in a chamber and dissolve the calcareous material within it. As the material dissolves, it gives up calcium and magnesium, which is pumped into the main tank for the corals to use. Don't forget that you'll need a fully functional pressurised CO_2 kit just as you would in a freshwater planted aquarium, and most are best fitted to a sump. Calcium reactors are favoured by hobbyists who have lots of fast-growing, reef-building corals, with high demands on calcium and magnesium. Once bought and fitted, they can have lower annual running costs than liquid calcium supplements.

■ Ultraviolet steriliser (UV) – not to be confused with an ultraviolet clarifier for ponds, a UV is similar but uses a much finer void space to zap disease pathogens as well as unicellular algae. By killing off free-floating disease organisms, the fish are less likely to host diseases. As has been mentioned, UVs are commonly used to keep marine Whitespot at bay on surgeonfish. You'll need a powerhead to run a UV, or an external filter. Choose the model rated for your aquarium volume or larger, and for best results change the UV tube every six months. It's important for your safety that you don't look directly at a

UV tube when it's illuminated, as it could harm your eyes, and when changing UV bulbs wear gloves or hold them in tissue paper so that no oils from your skin come into contact with the surface.

Marine décor

Marine décor is usually quite different to freshwater decor, and almost always has its origins in the sea. Both rock and sand décor are usually calcareous, which benefits the marine aquarium's water parameters.

Coral sand

Coral sand is made up of the tiny broken pieces of coral and shell that are found around reefs. With abrasion these become finer and finer, and after being sieved and graded by aquatic suppliers coral sand typically has a grain size of between 1–3mm. Being calcareous, it benefits marine water and helps to buffer pH, alkalinity and calcium levels. See also page 35.

Aragonite

Aragonite also consists of the fine rubble and sand that's found around reefs. It looks similar to coral sand but is even better at buffering marine reef water parameters. When exposed to pH of less than 8.2 it dissolves, and being made up of coral skeletons it releases every element that the coral once possessed, to the benefit of the live corals in your aquarium.

This dissolving process takes time, and aragonite substrates normally need to be topped up just once or twice per year.

Usually available in a bright cream/white colour, aragonite comes in a variety of grain sizes from 3mm down to less than a millimetre. The very finest aragonite is called sugar-sized or oolitic sand, which with its high surface area provides the greatest buffering capacity. It looks good too. Bright white aragonite sands are said to benefit bright-light-loving corals, by reflecting light back up from the aquarium floor.

Live rock

The heart of every reef aquarium, live rock is rock that's been taken from the reef itself. Made up of highly porous dead coral skeletons, it becomes solid as a result of years of compression and the addition of further calcium deposits in and around it. It's called 'live' rock from being colonised by bacteria, both aerobic bacteria on the outside and anaerobic bacteria on the inside.

This biological activity is of great benefit to a reef aquarium, as in theory it can provide complete nitrification by breaking down ammonia and nitrite into nitrate, and by converting nitrate by means of the denitrifying anaerobic bacteria inside it. So it aids buffering, it can filter – rendering it a key element of the most widespread natural marine filtration system in the world, the Berlin system (see page 137) – and has other benefits too. Because it's not just alive with bacteria, but with a whole range of aquatic organisms too, from desirable macro algaes to sponges, fan worms, calcareous algaes, small crustaceans including detritivores, plankton, occasional coral polyps and just about anything else that can be found living on a natural reef.

This brings huge benefits to a reef aquarium, as just one lump of live rock adds a magnitude of diversity, and no décor looks better in a marine aquarium than mature live rock.

Available from several different geographic regions, and in different shapes and sizes, live rock likewise differs in density, the diversity of the life that's on it, and in structure. Generally the most desirable live rocks are those that are light in structure and porous, to encourage nitrification. Good coralline algae coverage is also desirable, though dead coral branches from storm damage are also popular (called 'branch rock' or 'reef bones'). A combination of several types from several locations will offer maximum shape, porosity and diversity.

See also pages 146–7.

Ocean rock

Used in both hard water freshwater set-ups and marine set-ups, ocean rock provides an instant marine-looking aquascape. It's heavy and dense, and is usually used either in fish-only set-ups or as a base upon which to place more expensive, more desirable live rock. It can help with buffering, though an aragonite substrate would be more effective. See also page 36.

Tufa

Not commonly used in marine aquariums these days, tufa is generally disregarded because of its crumbly nature and the fact that it can absorb and then release nitrate. It should be used in fish-only marine aquariums or not at all. See also page 36.

Replica live rock

Looking similar to the real thing, replica live rock is used to aid marine aquascapes either by bulking up heavy, expensive piles of rock, or by being glued into place to provide lightweight overhangs and caves that wouldn't normally be possible with the real thing.

Barnacle clusters

Marine in origin, giant barnacle clusters can be used in reef building, as decorative touches, or in order to provide homes for small fish such as gobies and blennies. They're safe for hard water freshwater tanks too.

Live rock

Live rock is absolutely essential to the modern reef aquarium as it has many benefits, which have been outlined on pages 150–1. Let's look at it in more depth, in order that you can make a more informed buying choice.

Types of live rock

Live rock comes in several forms. Essentially it all combines to make up the structure of a coral reef, but it can be made up from different coral skeletons, some from different depths, be of different ages, and derive from different parts of the world. This variety means that shape, structure, porosity, density and coralline algae coverage will vary.

Rock from Fiji was the most desirable for many years, as it was light when compared to its mass, and looked very desirable, being covered in lots of pink and purple algae. Indonesian rock is similar and seems to make up the bulk of rock sold today.

For something totally different, branch rock – sometimes called Pacific Ultra Branch, Tongan Branching Rock or reef bones – consists of pieces of Staghorn Coral broken off by

storms and collected from the edge of the reef. It's dense compared to Fijian rock and has very little internal surface area for bacteria to colonise, so it won't filter like the others, but the odd piece here and there can give a reef tank a natural look, and corals can then be stuck on it and will protrude out into open water.

Cultured rock is man-made rock manufactured from mined limestone or white cement which has been placed in the sea for a while to become seeded with live organisms and bacteria. A keen eye will be able to spot cultured rock, as it looks more regular and rounded in shape than natural live rock. Reports suggest that it may also not have the porosity of the real thing. Cultured rock is a greener option, though, as it means that the world's remaining natural reefs can be left intact.

Buying live rock

Live rock can seem expensive at first, being three or four times the price per kilo of dead base rocks such as tufa or ocean rock. However, the benefits are massive. It can even

become quite addictive, as after adding it to the tank it's fascinating to see the myriad of microscopic life radiate from it and turn your sparse, moon-like rock pile into a living ecosystem.

Visit all your local marine shops to get a feel for what's available, and look online too. Live rock will vary in price per kilo, maturity and quality, with the best being a large, light piece of Fiji, for example, with a good coverage of coralline algae and tiny added extras such as the odd coral polyp or tiny fan worms. A poor quality piece of live rock will be one that's very dense – meaning low porosity and a high price per kilo – and a light, almost cream colour with no visible signs of life on its surface at all.

Take your time choosing live rock, as this will be your filter as well as your décor. If you can't afford a large quantity, buy a piece per week or per month instead. In terms of the quantity necessary, advice will vary depending on whom you ask, but one kilo per ten litres of tank volume is a good guideline to start with. The more the better, but make sure that there's sufficient flow of water around it to keep the bacteria functioning properly.

Buy cured rock, meaning that it's matured, has been settled in a tank for several weeks and is ready to go.

Curing live rock

This is normally done for you, though there is a financial saving in buying uncured live rock. When live rock is taken from the ocean it's shipped dry, in cardboard boxes, meaning that lots of the microscopic aquatic life within it dies off in transit. It's shipped this way to keep the weight, and subsequently the price, down.

The unfortunate knock-on effect of transportation is that if you then placed newly transported rock into your aquarium all the dead stuff in and around it would foul the water, causing lots of pollution and unstable water conditions.

Newly shipped live rock therefore usually goes through a process of cleaning, cleansing and re-maturing. This is called curing. It normally involves the rock being placed in a vat with high circulation, aeration and plenty of water-changes to get rid of the dead stuff and encourage regrowth of the live stuff. Large, industrial-sized protein skimmers help in the waste removal process. The whole process normally takes about three weeks, which incurs significant costs.

If you buy an unopened box of rock just as it is when it comes into the airport, however, no curing has been done and you can buy it cheaper. But you then have to go through the rinsing, water changing and heavy protein skimming process for the next few weeks in order to cure it yourself.

Sniff your rock!

If you're unsure if live rock is cured or uncured, give it a sniff. Cured rock will smell sweet and inviting, like fresh seafood. Uncured rock will smell musty and dirty. Only if live rock smells good will it have been cured.

Types of marine tank

Just as with freshwater aquariums, marine aquariums can be set up in a number of ways, and to house different species.

There are three main types of marine aquarium to focus on, each with its own benefits. These are fish-only, fish-only with live rock, and reef. Between these three types it should be possible to keep every available marine organism, space permitting.

Fish-only

As its name suggests, a fish-only marine aquarium contains just fish, and, usually, decoration. This is probably the oldest practised marine aquarium style, as in the early days of the hobby marine fish were kept much more successfully than corals; and because corals and invertebrates aren't included in a fish-only marine tank, fish species that would normally predate them can also be housed.

Pros
In a fish-only aquarium the fish are the stars, and you have

the greatest choice of fish species. Also, you only need to look after the needs of the fish instead of worrying about lighting and calcium levels etc, so it's less technical, and generally fish are hardier than invertebrates and more tolerant of nitrate being present in the water.

Phosphate doesn't harm fish, so this is also less of a priority than with a reef, and you get to stock more fish per volume than a reef, as ultra-low nutrient values are less important. Salinity is less important too in a fish-only aquarium, and with no invertebrates present salt levels can actually be reduced quite significantly in order to keep marine diseases such as Whitespot at bay. You can also use copper-based medications that would normally kill all invertebrates, but are much more effective at eradicating parasites.

Cons
The majority of fish-only species, such as triggers, puffers etc, eat copious amounts of fish and shellfish, producing rich waste. This requires strong filtration and large water-changes to stop nitrate from reaching dangerous levels. The sorts of fish that are generally mixed in fish-only aquariums

do tend to be the more aggressive species too, such as damselfish and large angelfish species, so fighting is more likely.

Also although they may be classed as 'fish-only' fish, many species – such as butterflyfish, for example – are specialised feeders and may not be best suited to the barren conditions of a fish-only aquarium, or the raised levels of stocking and aggression.

Fish-only with live rock

Abbreviated to FOWLR, this sort of system is a more modern version of the fish-only marine aquarium.

Pros
The addition of live rock gives more potential for natural-looking aquascapes and provides natural hiding places and grazing areas for marine fish such as tangs, butterflyfish and angelfish. Live rock will bring with it small quantities of macro algae, zooplankton and sponges, which will supplement the diet of the grazers and provide them with environmental enrichment as they search the rock pile for food.

Cons
The addition of live rock will bump up the price of the whole system, and if you use an external filter and live rock then nitrate production and subsequent water-changes will be high.

If large wrasses, puffers and triggers are included in the FOWLR system they'll crunch up the rock with their powerful teeth and remove the desirable coating of pink and purple coralline algae, so it could end up looking quite barren and not resemble the rich colours of a reef at all.

Reef

With the reef aquarium, you're setting out to create your own miniature slice of a natural coral reef.

Pros
You can't beat it for diversity, as in a reef aquarium everything is alive, from the rock upwards. In terms of aesthetics too, watching your fish swimming through corals, and crabs, shrimps and starfish all interacting together, is a wonderful thing, and still one of the best aquarium vistas available.

Cons
The reef aquarium is often the most expensive side of the hobby, as significant investment has to be made in lighting, circulation, nutrient removal (ie a skimmer), live rock, test kits and livestock. Corals aren't cheap, and the average livestock list can be as expensive as the equipment and tank combined.

You get to stock less fish in a reef aquarium per volume, as you have to keep pollution to an absolute minimum at all times. The list of reef-safe species is prohibitive too, and some hobbyists feel that this excludes all the characterful, entertaining species, such as puffers.

Setting up an aquarium

Before you take the final plunge into marines, you must first accept that it's the most challenging area of the fishkeeping hobby, and that you have a responsibility to do the best that you can for the livestock involved, as the majority have been taken from the wild for the sole purpose of giving us viewing pleasure.

It can also be one of the most expensive sides of the hobby, and time-consuming, so if you can't devote the necessary time, research and financial resources, don't take it up.

Let's look again at the tropical marine environment, as the more that you know about it, the easier it will be to replicate

What corals need
- Light
- Water movement
- Low nutrient levels
- Stable water conditions
- Food

it and thus fulfil the needs of your marine tank inhabitants.

Coral reefs are found only in certain regions of longitude and latitude across the globe, and occur in very exacting

conditions. Their key requirement is a bright tropical sun that shines all day every day, almost without fail. By containing photosynthetic algae lots of the corals on reefs have even learnt to use the sun as an additional source of food.

Another reason why the sun is so important to a reef is the crystal clear water. Reefs don't exist anywhere that turbid water is found because no light penetration means no food for the corals.

Finally, reefs exist in areas of high water movement. This movement brings the coral food in the form of zooplankton, and washes away its waste products. The water around a thriving coral reef is consequently always very low in nutrients and very stable all year round.

The coral builds reef structures, which in turn provide food and shelter for fish, and so the ecosystem is complete.

Creating marine conditions

Bearing in mind what corals need, and that the fish are very similar in their requirements – only less demanding of light, of course – you can now go on to create your own marine aquarium.

Light
Bright sunlight-like lighting will require either multiple T5, metal halide or multiple LED lighting, all in the correct marine spectrums. Duration is also important, so set the lights to ten hours per day, every day.

Water movement
This is easily achieved by powerheads or circulation pumps. A turnover of 20 times per hour is a good average, so calculate 20 times tank volume (*ie* 4000lph for a 200-litre tank) and then obtain a pump (or realistically two in this case) to match.

Low nutrients
This is just as important as the first two requirements, only more difficult to attain on a consistent basis. When we refer to nutrients in a marine environment we're referring to the levels of nitrates and phosphates which build up from filtration, fish waste and fish food. They need to be kept as close to zero as possible.

Even live rock creates a certain amount of nutrients, but it should deal with ammonia and nitrite, and water-changes will deal with nitrate. A protein skimmer will help to remove all nutrients and a refugium can help to remove nitrates and phosphates, albeit slowly. Phosphate has no effect whatsoever on fish but is very detrimental to corals, so should be removed by chemical means using a phosphate-removing resin.

Stable water conditions
Stable water conditions means stable temperature, stable salt levels and stable low nutrient levels. High temperatures

will kill corals and other invertebrates and stress everything in the tank. The cause of high temperatures will most likely be powerful lighting, so calculate the trade-off between, say, having the brightest metal halide lighting but then having to pay out on fans or expensive cooling equipment. Chillers should really be a compulsory item, only they're expensive to buy, expensive to run and aren't very green. The livestock's immediate requirements for stable temperatures must come first, however.

Bright light and warm temperatures will also cause evaporation, with some 25 litres per week being normal. Evaporation of freshwater from salt will cause salt levels to increase in the tank, again causing stress and instability. Be prepared to top up regularly – daily in some cases – or shell out on an automatic top-up device that will do it for you. The need to keeping those nutrients levels low has already been mentioned.

Food

And just as you're ready to give it all up before you've even started there's the equally important issue of food. You could have the best flow, the best light and the purest water, but without food your corals will still starve.

Proper feeding has been one of the major breakthroughs in coral-keeping over the past decade. Corals feed in two ways: by means of symbiotic algae within them and by using their polyps to catch food that drifts past. Their food ranges from tiny plant-like phytoplankton to larger animal zooplankton. Both available from your marine specialist retailer.

As for marine fish, the coral reef environment is one of the best examples in nature of specialisation. The abundance of potential food sources on a reef varies immensely for fish, from eating each other to eating algae, corals or even parasites on other fish. The specialised feeders on the reef have an edge over competitors, as it means that they can get by on foodstuffs that the others can't eat. Place a specialised fish in a reef aquarium, however, with controlled stocking and a limited supply of its natural foods, and you may have a problem.

Research the feeding requirements of all your potential purchases and avoid those specialised feeders that you can't provide for. Keep a tank of healthy disease-free fish, for example, and a Cleaner Wrasse will have nothing to eat. However, keep a dwarf angel, which can survive on meaty foods, plant foods and even manufactured foods, and it will find life much easier.

To sum up…

Hopefully the above will give you an idea of what marines need day to day. Buy the right kit in the first place and life will be much easier in the long run, even if it seems more expensive at the time. Marine conversions, where freshwater

set-ups are changed to marine, are often compromises in terms of the amount of light that you can add to them, the type of nutrient control that you use and the equipment that you can fit, and they can be a false economy.

Although conversions bring many existing hobbyists into marines, if you have a freshwater systemised tank on which you then upgrade the lighting and filtration, and even take a hacksaw to the hood in order to fit extra equipment, you must ask yourself if there was any point – and indeed, any saving – in not simply investing in the right marine tank in the first place.

The best marine tanks are those that have been planned properly, and use equipment that's been proven to do the intended job.

Nano marine tanks

No part of the hobby, either freshwater or marine, has grown as quickly as the nano market. Nano tanks, or small tanks per se, aren't new, as we've always had them. A goldfish bowl could even be considered the original nano environment. The big change, however, is what we do with them, and what's available for them.

A nano marine tank can now be equipped with a nano light, a nano skimmer, a nano circulation pump and even nano fish, being a perfect working – but smaller – replica of a traditional reef tank. They take up much less space, they're much cheaper to set up and run, as they use less of everything and are cheaper to stock.

Before you rush out to buy a nano aquarium, however, they do have their limitations. Going back to the requirements of reef life, stability is a big limiting factor for nano tanks, as they heat up and cool down more quickly. Nutrients can be controlled effectively by large

regular water-changes, but small tanks become polluted more quickly too. And think about the choice of livestock for a minute. Despite the variety of marine fish available in the shops, you'll be significantly limited by size. A nano shouldn't contain any fish over about 5cm in length, and the more you have in there the more quickly the pollutants will build up.

Some corals will even get too big for a nano. So ask yourself if, despite everything seeming so much cheaper and more convenient, a nano will actually enable you to create a stunning marine vista teeming with life?

Nano marine aquariums definitely have their place, but they lack the wow factor of a large reef aquarium.

Reef tank step-by-step

1 The empty tank and cabinet. Choose as large a tank as you can, as larger bodies of water are more stable (which is very important for marines). It also means more room for corals and aquascaping and valuable swimming space for desirable species such as tangs.

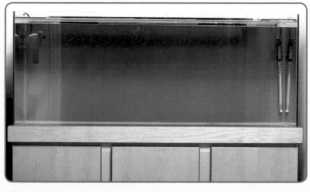

2 Fit the heater and the circulation pumps. Aim for a turnover of at least ten times per hour if you're keeping soft corals, and twenty times per hour for hard corals. In this instance the heater and circulation pumps will also be used to mix up the salt.

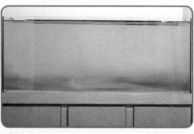

3 Fill the tank with RO water from the start, which is free of nitrates and phosphate. Turn the pumps and heater on to warm and circulate the water around the tank. Wait until the water is at 24°C before the next step.

4 Pour marine salt into the tank and let the pumps circulate it until it dissolves. The box or bucket that the salt comes in will say how much saltwater it will make, so buy enough and use slightly less than is required, so that you can top up the last bit gradually and get an accurate reading.

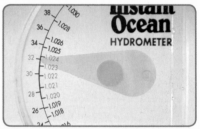

5 Use a hydrometer to measure the salt content of the water. This model has a red safety zone indicated, and will be calibrated to read salt levels at 24°C. If the water is too salty, remove some and add fresh. If it's not salty enough, add more salt and wait for it to dissolve fully before taking another reading.

6 Add some base rock (optional) to bulk up the live rock pile and begin to shape the reef. This spaghetti rock is open and porous like live rock, and is safe to use with marines. The idea is that base rock is much cheaper per kilo than live rock, and it will be hidden by live rock on top.

7 Add live rock to the tank, placing it on top of the base rock. Lean it against the back glass and place it carefully, building a sturdy pile that will soon make a platform upon which to grow corals. Use large pieces at the bottom and smaller pieces on the top. Give the pile a final shake to make sure that it's sturdy and won't slide or fall down.

8 If you're using the Berlin method of filtration (live rock, water circulation and a protein skimmer) the skimmer should be added next. This hang-on-the-back model is powerful and remains conveniently out of the way. Run the skimmer 24 hours per day and clean the collection cup regularly.

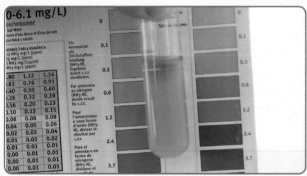

9 Once the live rock is in place, proper maturation can begin. Even cured rock may have some residues of ammonia and phosphate so the skimmer is used to remove any leached waste. Test the water daily for the first few weeks to check for traces of ammonia and nitrite. No livestock should be added if there are any traces of either compound.

10 Once matured, the first fish can be added, which in this case is a hardy clownfish. Again test the water for ammonia and nitrite over the next few weeks and only add further fish if they remain at zero. Feed sparingly so as not to pollute the tank early on.

11 Invertebrates such as hermit crabs, snails and hardy soft corals can be added after an extended period of stable water conditions. Phosphate-removing resin should be added when the corals go in, to keep levels as low as possible.

12 The finished tank, full of life and well on its way to resembling a full-blown natural reef. As the next few weeks and months go by, more fish and corals can be added.

Buying marine fish

Buying the right marine fish for your tank can be more complicated than you think. Unlike freshwater fish, they all require the same water parameters and levels of salt, the biggest challenge being that of compatibility.

Choice

As has already been said, marine fish offer a huge amount of choice and variety, and they're so colourful and so stunning that when they're all viewed together in an aquatic shop choosing the right fish for your own tank can be a bit overwhelming. Make the choice right, and you'll get years of colour, movement and entertaining behaviour from them. Get it wrong, and your dream of a tranquil slice of a coral reef in your living room could be destroyed.

Reef or fish-only

Tropical marine fish are divided into those that will live in harmony with corals and mobile invertebrates such as shrimp, and those that will try to eat them. Your aquarium must already be set up and matured before you even think about buying the first fish, so by the time you step foot into the aquatic shop you should have a clear idea of what you'll be keeping – reef fish or fish-only fish.

This will cut the choice of available fish in half, as all the butterflyfish, triggerfish and large wrasses will be out of bounds to reef-keepers, while it's very uncommon to keep small reef-compatible fish in a sparsely decorated fish-only tank. A good retailer will normally have a labelling system that will indicate whether a fish is fish-only or reef, and sometimes the two types will be displayed only with others of their own kind, or even in different tank systems.

Do your research

Get an idea of the fish species you want to keep before you buy them, by looking at the fish profiles listed on pages 166–73. Due to the nature of the marine hobby and its extreme diversity of species, there will nearly always be a fish that you've never seen before, even for many experts. But bear in mind that if it isn't listed in the profiles it won't be that common, and there may be a reason for that, such as they're difficult to keep alive in captivity, have a remote distribution or could be aggressive. Rarely will you find an unheard-of fish that will make a perfect reef specimen. Don't buy any fish that you know nothing about. It could be a huge mistake.

Explain your wants to a member of staff

Once you have an idea of what you want, find a member of staff who specialises in marines. Explain to them that you have a newly set-up tank, give them details of its dimensions and equipment, and say whether it's intended to be fish-only or reef. Then tell them which fish you'd like to buy.

A good member of staff should be well versed in this kind of situation and will probably talk to you about water tests and results, or ask you to bring some water in for them to test before you take any fish. They should then be able to say whether the fish that you've shortlisted fish are suitable for your tank, are compatible with each other long-term, and in what order they should be added. All reef tanks under six months old should be regarded as still new, so fish should be added with caution. During this time you should be choosing hardier species rather than the more difficult ones, and a sign of a good retailer will be one whose staff echo that, by recommending a tank-bred clownfish, for example, rather than a regal tang.

Make sure that they're healthy

If you haven't kept any kind of fish before this won't be easy, but if you're experienced in keeping freshwater fish, the same signs apply. Most marine fish should be actively swimming in mid-water unless they're adapted to live on the bottom. The eyes should be clear and the fins erect, and colours should be clearly defined and bold.

Two big things to look out for are firstly that the fish is feeding, and secondly that it doesn't have any signs

of marine Whitespot. Ask a member of staff to demonstrate that the fish is eating before you take it. This is less important for a tank-bred clownfish that's known for not being a picky eater, but very important for a butterflyfish or even a lionfish that's come straight from the wild and may still be too scared and too shocked to eat anything. Any fish that won't feed in front of you should be left in the shop until it can be demonstrated that it's settled and is accepting marine foods.

Whitespot, both freshwater and marine, manifests itself as a covering of tiny white spots all over the fish. This is highly contagious, can be fatal, and yet is very difficult to eradiate from a reef tank. Again, don't buy any fish that has even one tiny white spot on its skin. See also page XXX.

Copper

Copper in its liquid form is commonly used in the treatment of marine diseases. It's effective because it's toxic to marine parasites and will kill them. Those parasites are actually tiny invertebrates, and they and larger inverts like your corals and ornamental inverts will all be wiped out by even tiny amounts of copper introduced to the marine tank.

Ask your retailer if they have copper medications in with their marine fish, as many do to destroy parasites. If you have a fish-only marine aquarium with no live rock then it's fine to introduce some copper to your home aquarium – it will even help keep away parasite infestations – but if you have a reef tank it's lethal. Always check and make shop staff well aware that you have a reef tank before you purchase fish.

Introducing marine fish

If you've bought just a few fish they'll normally be transported home in plastic bags inside a brown paper bag and then a carrier bag. Larger fish or larger quantities will usually travel in plastic bags inside a sealed polystyrene box.

Acclimatising

Marine organisms are sensitive to change, so it's important to make their introduction into your tank as smooth as possible.

Acclimatising freshwater fish was covered on pages 72 and 73, where the drip method and the much more common floating bag method were both described. Of these, the drip method is by far the best for marine fish and invertebrates, which require slow and seamless acclimatisation.

Why the drip method is better for acclimatising marines

- Slower acclimatisation makes for a more stress-free introduction.
- Water conditions and salt levels will mix more slowly.
- The fish are acclimatised to the water away from the main tank, so that once introduced they only have to concentrate on setting up home.
- All bag water can be discarded with no risk of contamination.
- If the fish is removed with a net, even copper-based water from the aquatic shop won't be introduced to your main tank, so the risk of copper poisoning is greatly reduced.

Drip acclimatisation step-by-step

2 Open the fish bags and release the fish into the bottom of the bucket. Due to the small amount of bag water there won't be much in the bucket to start off with, but as long as the fish's back is covered with

water it'll be fine. If several fish have come from the same shop, and importantly the same tank system, then several fish can be acclimatised in the same bucket at the same time. If fish have come from different water sources, several buckets should be used, or one fish should be acclimatised after the other.

1 First find a clean bucket – the one that you change water with will be fine, but one with a snap-top lid will be even better. If it has a lid, drill a small hole in it about 12–25mm in diameter. This is where the airline will poke through into the bucket, so that air can travel freely between the bucket and the atmosphere.

3 Next you need some airline. This is the stuff that's connected to air pumps and airstones, and every aquatic shop sells it. You will need about 2m to get from the top of the aquarium to the bucket on the floor. Buy an in-line air control valve at the same time.

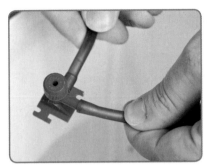

4 Cut the airline and connect the in-line tap. This will allow you to control the flow of water from the tank to the bucket.

5 Place one end of the airline in the marine tank and secure it with an algae magnet or airline clip and rubber sucker, so that it can be left hanging from the tank and won't fall off.

6 Start a siphon going from the tank to the bucket by sucking the pipe. Water should start to flow into the bucket. If a snap-top lid with a hole is used, poke the airline through the hole. A lid is very useful for stopping fish from jumping out of the bucket.

7 Slowly adjust the in-line control valve so that the water is turned down from a trickle to a drip of about one droplet of water per second.

8 Leave for half an hour to an hour, in which time the small amount of water in the bucket containing the fish will change from 100 per cent shop water to about 90 per cent tank water.

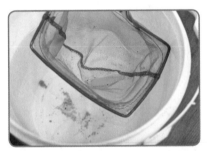

9 Catch the fish with a net and place into the main tank. Always have the lights turned off for an hour when introducing new fish.

10 Discard the water in the bucket, as it will have traces of pollution from the fish transportation water.

11 Top up the water in the main tank, turn the lights back on – with the blue actinics coming on first if you have the option – and observe the newly introduced fish. Some marine fish will hide for several days before coming out into the open.

INTRODUCING MARINE FISH

165

Marine fish profiles

Green Chromis

Scientific name	Chromis viridis.
Origin	Indo-Pacific.
Size	7.5cm.
Tank size	100cm.
Tank type	Reef or fish-only.
Ease of keeping	Easy.
Swimming level	Top.
Feeding	Flakes, Mysis, krill and Brine Shrimp.
Breeding	Isn't bred commercially, and any aquarium spawnings are accidental.
Special requirements	Groups.

Notes – Green Chromis are very peaceful as damselfish go, and one of the best-behaved reef fish available. They never touch corals or invertebrates and are constantly active. They do need to be kept in groups of five or more, which combined with their activity means that they need a roomy tank.

Common Clownfish

Scientific name	Amphiprion ocellaris.
Origin	Indo-West Pacific.
Size	10cm.
Tank size	60cm.
Tank type	Reef or fish-only.
Ease of keeping	Moderate.
Swimming level	Middle.
Feeding	Marine flakes, frozen Brine Shrimp, Mysis and krill
Breeding	Can be bred in the aquarium, though the fry are difficult to raise and die due to lack of food or being taken in by the filtration.
Special requirements	Wild Common Clowns should be given a host anemone.

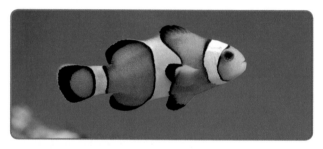

Notes – Known by novices as Disney's Nemo, the Common Clown is a peaceful, pair-forming reef fish that naturally lives within an anemone. In captivity, tank-bred Clowns don't need an anemone, though they'll usually take to one within weeks or months of it being introduced. Tank-bred Clowns are recommended as one of the best species to start off with in marines, though they're prone to jumping from open-topped tanks. The Percula Clownfish is a very similar species.

Royal Gramma

Scientific name	Gramma loreto.
Origin	Western Central Atlantic.
Size	7cm.
Tank size	60cm.
Tank type	Reef.
Ease of keeping	Moderate.
Swimming level	Middle.
Feeding	Frozen Brine Shrimp, Mysis, krill and zooplankton.
Breeding	Has not been bred in captivity.
Special requirements	Live rock caves.

Notes – Royal Grammas have stunning colouration, and that combined with their reef-safe nature and small size makes them popular additions to a reef aquarium. They're cave-dwellers, which need a bolthole in the live rock to feel

secure. Once they've taken up residence they'll defend it against other small reef fish.

Banggai Cardinal

Scientific name	*Pterapogon kauderni*.
Origin	Western Central Pacific, Banggai Islands.
Size	8cm.
Tank size	100cm.
Tank type	Reef.
Ease of keeping	Moderate.
Swimming level	Middle.
Feeding	Frozen krill and Mysis.
Breeding	Can be bred in the aquarium. Males are mouthbrooders, and the fry are large and relatively easy to care for when spat. If a group is left in a well-furnished aquarium without predators, many fry may survive.
Special requirements	None.

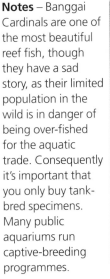

Notes – Banggai Cardinals are one of the most beautiful reef fish, though they have a sad story, as their limited population in the wild is in danger of being over-fished for the aquatic trade. Consequently it's important that you only buy tank-bred specimens. Many public aquariums run captive-breeding programmes.

Yellow Tang

Scientific name	*Zebrasoma flavescens*.
Origin	Pacific Ocean, Hawaii.
Size	15cm.
Tank size	120cm.
Tank type	Reef.
Ease of keeping	Moderate.
Swimming level	All levels.
Feeding	Algae, seaweed (nori), frozen Brine Shrimp, Mysis, Cyclops and krill.
Breeding	Has not been bred in the aquarium, and isn't bred commercially. Group-spawning egg-scatterer.
Special requirements	Live rock upon which to graze, swimming space.

Notes – Yellow Tangs are bright, beautiful reef fish and are very popular. They're very active and perform a useful role by grazing algae from live rock. One of the most peaceful of the tangs, and one of the easiest to keep, they should be kept singly in tanks of less than 150cm length, and in groups to form stunning displays in larger aquariums.

Regal Tang

Scientific name	*Paracanthurus hepatus*.
Origin	Indian Ocean.
Size	20cm.
Tank size	120cm.
Tank type	Reef.
Ease of keeping	Moderate.
Swimming level	All levels.
Feeding	Algae, frozen marine foods.
Breeding	Has not been bred in the aquarium, and isn't bred commercially. Group-spawning egg-scatterer.
Special requirements	A quarantine period, regular feeding in a reef environment, swimming space.

Notes – With their deep blue colouration and constant activity Regal Tangs are stunning fish for the reef aquarium. They should be kept singly in tanks of 120cm, though they can be kept in groups in much larger tanks. Unfortunately Regal Tangs are prone to Whitespot infections, especially small specimens, so quarantine for a period before introducing them to the main tank, and as an extra precaution install a UV steriliser.

Blue Damsel

Scientific name	*Chrysiptera cyanea.*
Origin	Indo-West Pacific.
Size	7.5cm.
Tank size	90cm.
Tank type	Reef or fish-only with live rock.
Ease of keeping	Easy.
Swimming level	All levels.
Feeding	Marine flakes, marine frozen foods.
Breeding	May spawn in the aquarium, though it's rarely raised or commercially bred. Pair-forming egg-depositor.
Special requirements	Tough tank-mates.

Notes – Blue Damsels are inexpensive, hardy and very colourful. They're safe with all invertebrates and corals, and even stay small, which should make them the perfect reef fish. The only problem with them – and it's quite a big

problem – is that they become territorial and aggressive shortly after being introduced. This can make life difficult for smaller, more sensitive reef fish, so they should be left out of most reef communities, or introduced in large groups to large aquariums with large, robust fish.

Blue Neon Goby

Scientific name	*Elactinus oceanops.*
Origin	Western Central Atlantic.
Size	5cm.
Tank size	60cm.
Tank type	Reef.
Ease of keeping	Moderate.
Swimming level	Bottom.
Feeding	Small frozen foods, zooplankton.
Breeding	Can be bred in the aquarium and is commercially bred. Pair-forming egg-depositor.
Special requirements	Corals amongst which to take up residence.

Notes – Blue Neon Gobies are interesting small reef fish that are suitable for nano reefs too. They're straightforward to

keep and may even breed, making them suitable candidates for a sustainable low impact reef. They may take on a fish-cleaning role too, acting like a cleaner wrasse for larger fish.

Yellow Goby

Scientific name	*Gobiosoma okinawae.*
Origin	Western Pacific, Japan.
Size	3.5cm.
Tank size	40cm and above.
Tank type:	Reef, nano reef.
Ease of keeping	Moderate.
Swimming level	Bottom.
Feeding	Small frozen foods, zooplankton.
Breeding	Can be bred in the aquarium and is bred commercially. Pair-forming egg-depositor.
Special requirements	Reef environment, non-territorial tank-mates.

Notes – These small gobies are very colourful, and are suitable for the nano reef as well as standard-sized

aquariums. They naturally inhabit corals in the wild, so this should be replicated in the aquarium, and they should not be combined with large, boisterous or territorial reef fish. Keep the temperature below 25°C, as they won't tolerate high temperatures.

Green Goby

Scientific name	*Gobiodon histrio.*
Origin	Indo-West Pacific.
Size	3.5cm.
Tank size	40cm and above.
Tank type	Reef, nano reef.
Ease of keeping	Moderate.
Swimming level	Bottom.
Feeding	Small frozen foods, zooplankton.
Breeding	Can be bred in the aquarium, and is bred commercially. Pair-forming egg-depositor.
Special requirements	Corals, peaceful tank-mates.

Notes – Green Gobies are good candidates for the reef aquarium as they're peaceful and may breed. They naturally inhabit coral branches in the wild, and are straightforward to keep. Don't combine with boisterous or territorial reef fish.

Pyjama Wrasse, Sixline Wrasse

Scientific name	*Pseudocheilinus hexataenia.*
Origin	Indo-Pacific.
Size	7.5cm.
Tank size	60cm and above.
Tank type	Reef.
Ease of keeping	Moderate.
Swimming level	All levels.
Feeding	Frozen foods.
Breeding	May spawn in the aquarium, but is rarely if ever raised in captivity.
Special requirements	Live rock upon which to find food.

Notes – Pyjama Wrasses are interesting fish, which are also useful to the reef aquarium because they eat pest flatworms and bristleworms. They're constantly on the move, looking for food amongst the live rock, but don't take kindly to the introduction of other wrasses into their territory.

Mandarin

Scientific name	*Synchiropus splendidus.*
Origin	Western Pacific.
Size	7.5cm.
Tank size	90cm.
Tank type	Mature reef.
Ease of keeping	Difficult.
Swimming level	Bottom.
Feeding	Live marine foods, zooplankton, copepods, some frozen foods.
Breeding	Has been bred in the aquarium, and is commercially bred in limited quantities.
Special requirements	Mature reef aquariums with an abundance of live foods.

Notes – Mandarins are exquisite in both shape and pattern. Because of this they're very popular reef fish, though many people will lose their aquarium specimens due to long-term starvation. Mandarins need large expanses of sand and rubble that's crawling with live copepods and amphipods, on which they feed. The average reef tank doesn't produce enough of its own live food to support Mandarins, and other more competitive fish will take what live food there is before the Mandarins get to it. Any survival duration of less than a year should be considered a failure.

Coral Beauty

Scientific name	*Centropyge bispinosa.*
Origin	Indo-Pacific.
Size	10cm.
Tank size	90cm.
Tank type	Reef.
Ease of keeping	Moderate.
Swimming level	All levels.
Feeding	Algae, flakes and frozen foods.
Breeding	Has not been bred in the aquarium or commercially.
Special requirements	Live rock for grazing.

Notes – Coral Beauties are lovely dwarf angels, and one of the least likely to harass tube worms and clams. They do best in a mature reef aquarium, where they'll graze the rocks for both plant and tiny animal life. They can be kept in pairs and mixed with other dwarf angels, though only in very large tanks. Other than that they should be the only angel in a tank.

Flame Angel

Scientific name	*Centropyge loricula.*
Origin	Pacific Ocean.
Size	10cm.
Tank size	90cm.
Tank type	Reef.
Ease of keeping	Moderate.
Swimming level	All levels.
Feeding	Flakes, frozen marine foods, algae.
Breeding	May spawn in the aquarium but hasn't been bred, and isn't bred commercially.
Special requirements	Live rock for grazing.

Notes – Flame Angels are stunning reef fish that are very popular, if somewhat expensive. Their behaviour is typical of dwarf angels, grazing in and around live rock almost constantly, looking for food. There's a small risk that they may nip at clams and tube worms, and they're best kept as the only dwarf angel in a small tank, or in pairs or mixed with other dwarf angels in very large tanks.

Emperor Angel

Scientific name	*Pomacanthus imperator.*
Origin	Indo-Pacific, Red Sea, Hawaii.
Size	Up to 40cm.
Tank size	180cm and above.
Tank type	Fish-only, or fish-only with live rock.
Ease of keeping	Difficult.
Swimming level	All levels.
Feeding	Algae, dry and frozen foods.
Breeding	Has not been bred in the aquarium, or commercially.
Special requirements	Space, excellent water quality, excellent food.

Notes – Emperor Angels are archetypal marine fish that are simply amazing to look at, though they're suitable for few marine aquariums. They grow large, can be aggressive, and will nip at corals, so should only be kept in large fish-only systems. They're available either as juveniles (with a different colour pattern) or as adults. Juveniles are easier to acclimatise, though when their pattern does change they may not develop the bright colours of wild adults, due largely to inadequate diet. Feed them on a varied diet.

Regal Angel

Scientific name	*Pygoplites diacanthus.*
Origin	Indo-Pacific, Red Sea.
Size	25cm.
Tank size	150cm.
Tank type	Reef or fish-only aquarium with live rock.
Ease of keeping	Difficult.
Swimming level	All levels.
Feeding	Flake, frozen marine foods, algae.
Breeding	Has not been bred in the aquarium or commercially.
Special requirements	Space, excellent water quality, and live rock for grazing.

Notes – Regal Angels are perhaps one of the most beautiful angelfish available, and some success has been achieved when combining them with corals, despite their previously being categorised as not reef-safe.

Copper Band Butterflyfish

Scientific name	*Chelmon rostratus.*
Origin	Western Pacific.
Size	20cm.
Tank size	120cm.
Tank type	Reef or fish-only with live rock.
Ease of keeping	Difficult.
Swimming level	All levels.
Feeding	Frozen and live marine foods.
Breeding	Has not been bred in the aquarium or commercially.
Special requirements	Excellent water quality, mature aquariums, and suitable foods.

Notes – Copper Bands are one of the easiest to keep of the butterflies, because they aren't a specialised sponge- or coral polyp-feeder. However, you must make sure that the specimens in the shops are accepting food and fully acclimatised to aquarium life before you take them home. Copper Bands are often put to good use in a reef aquarium, as they eat nuisance Aiptasia anemones, though they may also nip at tube worms.

Scarlet Hawkfish

Scientific name	*Neocirrhites armatus.*
Origin	Pacific Ocean.
Size	8cm.
Tank size	90cm.
Tank type	Reef or fish-only with live rock.
Ease of keeping	Moderate.
Swimming level	Bottom.
Feeding	Meaty frozen foods.
Breeding	Has not been bred in the aquarium or commercially.
Special requirements	Live rock upon which to perch.

Notes – Hawkfish are small predatory fish that perch upon rocks and corals and watch life go by. They have quite a comical look on their faces and an entertaining swimming action, hopping around the aquarium as they go. They're reef-safe, though large specimens may eat tiny reef fish and shrimps. May sometimes jump.

Volitans Lionfish

Scientific name	*Pterois volitans.*
Origin	Pacific Ocean.
Size	35cm.
Tank size	180cm.
Tank type	Fish-only or reef with no small fish and no mobile invertebrates.
Ease of keeping	Moderate.
Swimming level	Middle.
Feeding	Frozen fish, frozen shellfish.
Breeding	Has not been bred in the aquarium, or commercially.
Special requirements	Meaty foods.

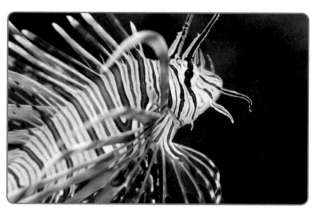

Notes – Lionfish are instantly recognisable, and the Volitans is probably the most popular species kept in aquariums, and one of the easiest to keep. They need large, wide aquariums because, with their fins spread out, they're as wide and as tall as they are long. They can be kept with corals but will eat anything moving that's small enough to be eaten. All lionfish are venomous, so care must be taken when catching them or cleaning the tank. Because of the risk, they should not be kept in a home aquarium if children are around.

Dwarf Fuzzy Lionfish

Scientific name	*Denrochirus brachypterus.*
Origin	Indo-West Pacific.
Size	15cm.
Tank size	90cm.
Tank type	Reef with no small fish or invertebrates, or fish-only with live rock.
Ease of keeping	Moderate.
Swimming level	Bottom.
Feeding	Frozen fish, frozen shellfish.
Breeding	Has not been bred in the aquarium, and isn't bred commercially.
Special requirements	Meaty foods.

Notes – Dwarf Fuzzy Lionfish are endearing to look at and reasonably easy to keep. They gorge themselves on frozen foods from a young age, and because of their low level of activity can be kept in fairly small aquariums, though with ample filtration to deal with their rich waste. Like all lionfish they're venomous, so should not be kept in a home aquarium if children are around, and care should be taken when cleaning their tank or catching them.

Porcupine Pufferfish

Scientific name	*Diodon holocanthus.*
Origin	Widespread across many tropical oceans.
Size	Up to 50cm.
Tank size	180cm and above.
Tank type	Fish-only.
Ease of keeping	Moderate.
Swimming level	All levels.
Feeding	Meaty foods, shellfish in shell.
Breeding	Has not been bred in the aquarium, or commercially.
Special requirements	Shellfish in their shells, to keep their teeth worn down.

Notes – Porcupine Pufferfish are so endearing to look at that they're very popular, though they do grow much larger than many people imagine. Their eyes move independently from one another, and they have almost cartoon-like characteristics when they swim. They're intelligent fish that will beg for food, though they're quite boisterous and should only be mixed with other boisterous fish, and preferably no other pufferfish. Inflation, showing off their spines, happens occasionally, but should not be encouraged through stressing the animal.

Picasso Triggerfish

Scientific name	*Rinecanthus aculeatus.*
Origin	Indo-Pacific.
Size	Up to 30cm.
Tank size	180cm.
Tank type	Fish-only.
Ease of keeping	Moderate.
Swimming level	All levels.
Feeding	Frozen fish, frozen shellfish in shell.
Breeding	Has not been bred in the aquarium.
Special requirements	Space, good filtration, and meaty foods.

Notes – The Picasso Triggerfish is exquisitely patterned and shaped, and is a popular fish for the fish-only aquarium. It's bold and active, though not as aggressive as its cousin the Clown Triggerfish, nor as expensive. Triggerfish need lots of room to exercise, and environmental enrichment in the form of crabs and prawns in their shells to attack, and rockwork to explore. Heavy filtration is necessary to break down their rich waste.

Snowflake Moray Eel

Scientific name	*Echidna nebulosa.*
Origin	Indo-Pacific.
Size	Up to 100cm.
Tank size	180cm.
Tank type	Fish-only.
Ease of keeping	Moderate.
Swimming level	Bottom.
Feeding	Frozen fish, frozen shellfish.
Breeding	Has not been bred in the aquarium, or commercially.
Special requirements	Meaty foods, hiding places, a tight-fitting lid.

Notes – Snowflake Morays are one of the smallest, most colourful and easiest to accommodate of all the moray eels, despite still growing to a length of 100cm. Morays are very primeval feeders, that first smell the food and then attack it savagely, curling into a ball and holding it in its unforgiving, backward-facing teeth. It's not a fish that should be kept around children, as it's liable to bite and injure fingers, and it should always be fed using long-reach tongs. They're hardy and easy to feed once settled. They must have a hideaway in which to retreat.

Yellow Boxfish

Scientific name	*Ostracion cubicus.*
Origin	Indo-Pacific.
Size	Up to 45cm.
Tank size	180cm.
Tank type	Fish-only.
Ease of keeping	Difficult.
Swimming level	All levels.
Feeding	Frozen foods.
Breeding	Has not been bred in the aquarium.
Special requirements	A large, specialist set-up.

Notes – This is a classic example of a fish *not* to buy in the aquarium store. Nature could not come up with an odder-looking fish if it tried, with its cubic shape and colour pattern. As juveniles they look even cuter, resembling a dice in shape and size. There is a catch, though, or rather several catches, to keeping this species. Firstly, it can grow to 45cm in length, outgrowing all but the largest of aquariums, and becomes more elongated as it grows and starts to lose its cute, cubic shape. Secondly, it isn't reef-safe, limiting what you can keep it with. And thirdly, if stressed it can exude a toxin which can poison the whole tank, including itself.

Marine invertebrates

The marine hobby has a whole other dimension to it: the invertebrates. These are incredibly varied in form, shape and colour, and some hobbyists prefer to keep them in their own right, and use marine fish only to provide movement in the upper water layers.

Marine invertebrates can be broadly split into two types – those that can move, the mobile inverts; and those that can't, the sessile inverts. Mobile inverts include crabs, shrimps and starfish, and sessile inverts include corals. Some corals can move position, such as *fungia sp.* hard corals and anemones, but to keep things simple they've also been grouped with the sessile corals.

Mobile invertebrates

A popular name in the USA for all mobile inverts is critters, and that sums them up quite nicely. There are thousands of critters to choose from, some being more suitable for life in captivity than others. We think of the majority of critters as being safe with each other, and safe with corals, though not all are. Harlequin Shrimp (*Hymenocera picta*), for instance, are specialist feeders that dine only on live starfish, so in the main are unsuitable for life in aquariums. Then there are the large hermit crabs that are considered too destructive for reef aquariums, and the Dancing Shrimp (*Rhynchocinetes*

durbanensis) which as well as preying on nuisance Aiptasia anemones will also eat coral polyps.

Use the mobile invertebrate profiles on pages 176–9 to research whether or not some of the most commonly seen mobile invertebrates are suitable for your tank.

What you need to know about mobile inverts

Although added to many tanks as scavengers, mobile inverts will need feeding in their own right in the absence of their natural food. Mature aquariums are best for any invert, as are those that can contain live rock for hiding amongst and grazing.

No mobile invertebrate needs any form of special lighting, though they're all sensitive to salinity levels, temperature and nitrate levels. Water must be at its optimum at all times, and new purchases should always be acclimatised slowly. All invertebrates are sensitive to copper in an aquarium, so many fish disease treatments are lethal to them.

Sessile invertebrates

Corals are sessile invertebrates, and again they can be roughly split into two types, hard corals and soft corals. Hard corals are the reef-building corals and are so-named because

Below: Soft corals are good for beginners.

Below: Star polyps spread quickly and are easy to keep.

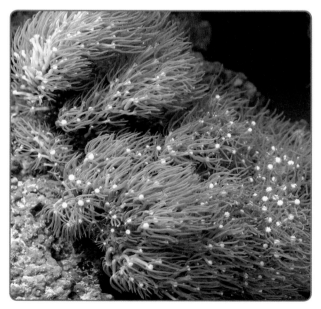

they form a hard, calcareous skeleton. Up until recently hard corals have nearly always been more difficult to keep than soft corals, requiring better water quality, stronger lighting and water flow in some circumstances, lower phosphate levels, and more specialised foods.

Hard corals

Hard corals are also known as stony corals, and can be further divided into large polyp stony corals and small polyp stony corals, or LPS and SPS for short. SPS represent the state of the art for many reef-keepers as they're the most demanding of all corals kept in aquariums. Conditions for SPS must be optimum at all times, often requiring extra equipment to be fitted, such as phosphate reactors and calcium reactors, and they demand the strongest water flow and brightest lighting of all. Staghorn Coral (*Acropora spp.*) typifies SPS corals.

LPS corals are beautiful, with nice colours and large fluorescent polyps in most cases, They require less flow and light than SPS, but need to feed more and are more aggressive, stinging each other and other corals at any opportunity. The coral specialist will often split LPS and SPS corals and grow them in separate conditions, in separate tanks. Bubble Coral (*Plerogyra spp.*) typifies LPS corals.

Soft corals

Soft corals don't create a hard internal skeleton like hard corals do, and are generally hardier, easier to keep and recommended for first-time reef-keepers. They range from tiny mats of coral polyps on the rocks, such as Green Star Polyps, to giant leather corals such as the toadstools. Mushrooms are one of the easiest families of soft corals to keep of all. To get the best out of them, still provide them with optimum water quality, even though they're much more tolerant of neglect and mistakes than the hard corals.

Above: LPS corals sway in the water current.

Below: Branching, Acropora corals should only be attempted by experienced reef keepers.

Below: Mushrooms are one of the best choices for new reef keepers.

Marine invertebrates

Turbo Snail

Scientific name	*Turbo fluctuosa.*
Origin	Mexico.
Size	5cm.
Tank size	40cm and above.
Ease of keeping	Moderate.
Feeding	Algae, detritus.
Breeding	May breed in the aquarium, with eggs being laid on the aquarium glass.
Special requirements	Algae.

Notes – Despite their name, Turbo Snails aren't fast movers,

but are of use to the reef hobbyist as algae grazers. As many as one per gallon of water can be stocked, but make sure that there's sufficient algae for them to graze to justify their introduction, otherwise they may starve. Don't let temperatures rise too high in summertime, as they won't tolerate it.

Red Leg Hermit Crab

Scientific name	*Paguristes cadenati.*
Origin	Indo-Pacific.
Size	2cm.
Tank size	40cm and above.
Ease of keeping	Easy.
Feeding	Algae, detritus, uneaten fish food.
Breeding	Has not been bred in the aquarium.
Special requirements	Spare shells.

Notes – Not to be confused with the Large Red-legged Hermit Crab, these ones are small and perform an important scavenging and grazing role in the reef aquarium. As many as one per gallon of water can be stocked, though they may try to kill Turbo Snails for their shells, or kill each other for their shells, so always provide more spare shells than there are crabs, and in a number of

different sizes. Blue-legged Hermit Crabs are similar, but even smaller.

Cleaner Shrimp

Scientific name	*Lysmata amboinensis.*
Origin	Indo-Pacific.
Size	7.5cm.
Tank size	60cm and above.
Ease of keeping	Moderate.
Feeding	All small marine fish foods.
Breeding	Has been bred commercially though rarely breeds in the home aquarium, although eggs are often released.
Special requirements	Slow acclimatisation.

Notes – Cleaner Shrimp are one of the most popular invertebrates in the hobby because of their bright colours and the way that they interact with fish, scouring their bodies for food. Sadly some become recluses after a period of time and may take up residence at the rear of the

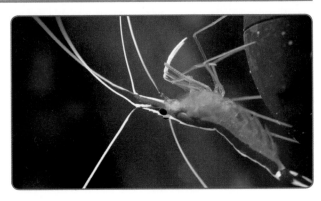

aquarium instead of coming out to be seen, though they will usually come out when the fish are being fed. They can be kept singly, in pairs or in groups, though slow acclimatisation is recommended as they're intolerant of changes in salinity and high temperatures.

Blood Shrimp

Scientific name	*Lysmata debelius.*
Origin	Indo-Pacific.
Size	5cm.
Tank size	60cm and above.
Ease of keeping	Moderate.
Feeding	Fish foods and food found on the surface of live rock.
Breeding	Has been bred in captivity and may spawn in the home aquarium, though eggs are rarely successfully raised by the hobbyist.
Special requirements	Slow acclimatisation.

Notes – Blood Shrimp rival Cleaner Shrimp in terms of their bright colours and good behaviour, though they may also start to hide away over time. Being reef-safe, they can be mixed with a large number of fish, corals and other mobile invertebrates and are a popular choice for the reef aquarium. Keep singly, in pairs or in groups, but acclimatise slowly as they're intolerant of changes in salinity and high temperatures.

Peppermint Shrimp

Scientific name	*Lysmata wurdemanni.*
Origin	Indo-Pacific.
Size	3cm.
Tank size	40cm and above.
Ease of keeping	Moderate.
Feeding	Aiptasia, small fish foods.
Breeding	Has been bred in captivity though is rarely raised by the home hobbyist.
Special requirements	None.

Notes – This small shrimp is popular in reef aquariums for one big reason – it predates nuisance Aiptasia anemones, which could ordinarily reach plague proportions and sting desirable corals in the process. First make sure that you get the right species, as there are many imposters that don't do want you intended. Add a group of them and try to tackle the really large Aiptasia yourself, as these small shrimp are more effective against small ones. Don't combine with any predatory fish.

Mithrax Crab, Emerald Crab

Scientific name	*Mithrax sculptus.*
Origin	Caribbean.
Size	2cm.
Tank size	40cm and above.
Ease of keeping	Moderate.
Feeding	Algae, small fish foods, food found on the surface of live rock.
Breeding	Has not been bred in captivity.
Special requirements	Live rock upon which to graze and in which to hide.

Notes – Mithrax crabs are used to control macro algae growths in reef aquariums, especially Bubble algae. You need to add several if they're to do their job successfully, as they're also partial to all others foods, especially fish food. They're reef-safe, and should be added as one of the janitors of a reef tank.

Sand Sifting Starfish

Scientific name	*Astropecten polycanthus.*
Origin	Fiji.
Size	15cm.
Tank size	90cm and above.
Ease of keeping	Moderate.
Feeding	Micro fauna within the sand.
Breeding	Has not been bred in the aquarium.
Special requirements	A large expanse of sand.

Notes – Sand Sifting Starfish are one the easiest starfish to keep, are reef-safe, and perform a useful role too. They burrow into the sand and turn it over as they search through it for food. Sometimes they'll disappear for weeks at a time. They need a sufficiently large bed of sand in which to forage, and the more mature the sand-bed the better, as it'll contain more food for them. Several can be added to large reef aquariums.

Boxing Shrimp

Scientific name	*Stenopus hispidus.*
Origin	Western Atlantic.
Size	10cm.
Tank size	90cm.
Ease of keeping	Moderate.
Feeding	Fish foods and food found amongst live rock.
Breeding	Has not been bred in the aquarium.
Special requirements	Hiding places.

Notes – Boxing Shrimp are popular, especially with new marine hobbyists, because of their exotic looks. They're fairly straightforward to keep, though some reports say that when they grow larger they can bully other shrimp species. They can be kept singly or in pairs, but have the unfortunate habit

of taking up residence behind live rock long-term, though they will come out at feeding time.

Blue Starfish

Scientific name	*Linckia laevigata.*
Origin	Papua New Guinea, Fiji, Indian Ocean.
Size	Up to 30cm diameter.
Tank size	90cm and above.
Ease of keeping	Difficult.
Feeding	Sponges.
Breeding	Has not been bred in captivity.
Special requirements	See below.

Notes – This starfish is absolutely stunning and many hobbyists will be tempted by it. However, it has a very poor survival rate in aquariums and should *not* be kept. It's a specialised feeder that feeds on sponges in the wild, and it travels and acclimatises incredibly badly. The few that do survive often start to disintegrate in a short time or exude their guts and then die. It may also be being over-collected for the aquatics trade.

Blue Legged Hermit Crab

Scientific name   Clibanarius tricolor.
Origin   Western Atlantic.
Size   2cm.
Tank size   30cm and above.
Ease of keeping   Moderate.
Feeding   Detritus, algae, leftover fish foods.
Breeding   Has not been bred in the aquarium.
Special requirements   Spare shells.

Notes – Blue Legged Hermits are even tinier than Red Legs, and can often be overlooked in shop tanks. They're straightforward to keep, though they should only be added to mature aquariums otherwise they may starve. Due to their diminutive size, other larger hermits may try to predate them if they get hungry so they're best kept as the only hermit in a reef tank. Provide spare shells and stock as many as one per gallon of aquarium water. A great species for nano tanks.

Arrow Crab

Scientific name   Stenorhynchus seticornis.
Origin   Western Atlantic.
Size   15cm.
Tank size   80cm and above.
Ease of keeping   Moderate.
Feeding   Leftover fish food, small invertebrates found amongst live rock.
Breeding   Has not been bred in the aquarium.
Special requirements   Live rock in which to hunt and find refuge.

Notes – Arrow Crabs have a unique look that some people love and others hate. Though they look quite dainty and fragile they're efficient predators and can easily hold their own in a reef tank. They're useful too as they eat bristleworms, though large females have also been known to predate small hermit crabs and even small fish. Consequently they've dropped out of fashion somewhat.

Brittlestar

Scientific name   Ophiarachna incrassata.
Origin   Indian Ocean.
Size   30cm diameter.
Tank size   120cm.
Ease of keeping   Moderate.
Feeding   Leftover fish food.
Breeding   Has not been bred in the aquarium.
Special requirements   Hiding places.

Notes – Brittlestars are great scavengers in the reef aquarium and they can get into all the nooks and crannies to find food. The green brittlestar is a common import, although it can get quite large and its frantic movements can unnerve small fish kept alongside it. It's therefore best to keep the tiny, free brittlestars that come in live rock. They will eat any dead or dying fish.

Marine coral profiles

Leather Coral, Toadstool

Scientific name	Sarcophyton spp.
Origin	Indo-Pacific.
Size	45cm.
Tank size	150 x 60 x 60cm.
Lighting	Moderate to bright.
Water flow	Moderate to high.
Ease of keeping	Moderate.
Special requirements	Space.

Notes – Toadstool coral is popular, readily available and fairly straightforward to keep. It grows rapidly in most circumstances, soon becoming too large for most standard-sized aquariums and casting a shadow over the corals underneath its large canopy. It spreads by producing offspring from its base.

Pulse Coral

Scientific name	Xenia spp.
Origin	Indo-Pacific.
Size	5cm tall.
Tank size	30cm and above.
Lighting	Moderate to bright.
Water flow	Low to high.
Ease of keeping	Easy.
Special requirements	None.

Notes – These are one of the easiest corals to keep, and they're also fascinating to watch. Their large polyps open and shut rhythmically, more so under bright lighting, and they spread rapidly if conditions are right. Because of its rapid spread, if elements are exhausted the colony may crash, disintegrating and remaining very small until conditions are right once more for a renewed population explosion. Very easy to propagate – just place rocks nearby and it will grow over them.

Finger Coral

Scientific name	Sinularia spp.
Origin	Indo-Pacific.
Size	45cm, depending on species.
Tank size	90cm.
Lighting	Moderate to bright.
Water flow	Moderate to high.
Ease of keeping	Moderate.
Special requirements	Space.

Notes – Finger Corals come in many colours, shapes and sizes, though their finger-like branches identify most. They're straightforward to keep and provide some vertical dimension to a soft coral tank. Like many soft coral species, they grow rapidly, to the point where they may outgrow some small reef aquariums.

Knobbly Mushroom

Scientific name	Ricordea spp.
Origin	Caribbean, Indo-Pacific.
Size	Up to 15cm across.
Tank size	40cm and above.
Lighting	Moderate to bright.
Water flow	Low to moderate.
Ease of keeping	Moderate.
Special requirements	Depends on species.

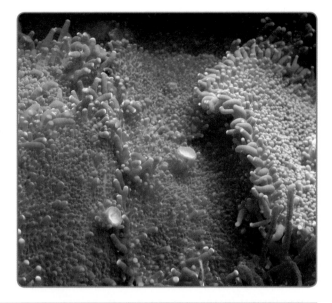

Notes – There are lots of different Knobbly Mushrooms available, either as colonies – usually of brown mushrooms known as Mushroom Rock – or very colourful, more desirable single mushrooms, known more commonly as Ricordea. The brown Mushroom Rocks are some of the easiest corals to keep and are tolerant of poor water conditions, poor light and poor flow. The single, more colourful species are much more difficult to keep and demand excellent water quality and good light.

Green Star Polyp

Scientific name	Pachyclavularia spp.
Origin	Indo-Pacific.
Size	1cm high.
Tank size	30cm and above.
Lighting	Moderate to bright.
Water flow	Moderate to high.
Ease of keeping	Moderate.
Special requirements	None.

Notes – Green Star Polyps are colourful and quite easy to keep. If conditions are right, they spread quickly over a purple-coloured base mat that can grow over rock and glass alike. To propagate, simply cut through the purple mat and attach it to another rock using an elastic band. In some circumstances growth can be so rampant that it can overgrow more difficult coral species.

Bubble Anemone

Scientific name	Entacmaea.
Origin	Indo-Pacific.
Size	40cm.
Tank size	120cm.
Lighting	Moderate to bright.
Water flow	Moderate to high.
Ease of keeping	Moderate.
Special requirements	A clownfish.

Notes – Anemones are popular because clownfish associate with them, but many people end up killing them. Specimens must be picked that are mostly brown in colour, as this shows that their zooxanthellae algae is intact, and they'll be able to use the aquarium lighting as a source of food. When placed in the aquarium, they'll find their own favoured spot, with adequate flow and light, and over a hole into which they can retreat. The perfect accompaniment for an anemone is a resident clownfish, as this will clean it, protect it and feed it. Anemones aren't as popular as they once were because of the way that they can walk through corals, stinging and even killing them as they go.

Staghorn Coral, Acropora

Scientific name	*Acropora spp.*
Origin	Indo-Pacific.
Size	Up to 60cm.
Tank size	80cm.
Lighting	Bright.
Water flow	High.
Ease of keeping	Difficult.
Special requirements	Bright light, strong water flow, low nutrient levels.

Notes – Acropora used to be thought impossible to keep in an aquarium, but in the past decade there have been many successes due to our better understanding of corals and their requirements, and the better lighting and water flow now provided in reef aquariums. Acropora are known as small polyp stony (SPS) corals because they build a hard skeleton. Cuttings can be taken and grown on, which is to be encouraged as it reduces the destruction of wild colonies. Acropora and other SPS need very low nutrient levels to survive.

Montipora

Scientific name	*Montipora spp.*
Origin	Indo-Pacific.
Size	60cm across.
Tank size	80cm.
Lighting	Bright.
Water flow	High.
Ease of keeping	Difficult.
Special requirements	Bright light, strong water flow, low nutrient levels.

Notes – Montipora are most well known as circular, plating SPS corals, although one species, *Montipora digitata*, looks more like an Acropora. Their shape and colour is highly desirable and they bring an authentic reef-look to any aquarium. They need strong light and water flow. though if they're placed too near to the surface they'll shade everything below them as they grow. Pieces can be broken off and grown on separately.

Bubble Coral

Scientific name	*Plerogyra spp.*
Origin	Indo-Pacific.
Size	30cm.
Tank size	60cm.
Lighting	Moderate.
Water flow	Moderate.
Ease of keeping	Moderate.
Special requirements	Space around them.

Notes – The Bubble Coral is one of the easiest of the large polyp stony (LPS) corals to keep, as it doesn't need such bright light and strong flow, and can feed itself by catching large food particles such as Brine Shrimp when the fish are being fed. It does have quite powerful sweeper tentacles, which it uses to fight and sting other corals that encroach on its space, so leave room around it.

Hammer Coral, Frogspawn Coral

Scientific name	Euphyllia spp.
Origin	Indo-Pacific.
Size	45cm.
Tank size	80cm.
Lighting	Moderate to bright.
Water flow	Moderate.
Ease of keeping	Moderate.
Special requirements	Space around them.

Notes – Hammer Coral and Frogspawn Coral belong to the Euphyllia family and are popular because of their fluorescent green polyp tips and the movement of the polyps in the water. Despite their looks they're actually quite aggressive LPS corals that send out long, powerful sweeper tentacles to sting other corals and to prevent being encroached on. This means that they need sufficient space all around them so that they can't fight with your other corals.

Sun Coral

Scientific name	Tubastrea spp.
Origin	Indo-Pacific.
Size	15cm.
Tank size	60cm.
Lighting	Low.
Water flow	Moderate.
Ease of keeping	Difficult.
Special requirements	Shade, meaty frozen foods.

Notes – Sun Corals are popular because of their bright orange colour, but most new marine keepers keep them entirely the wrong way. Sun Corals don't rely on sunlight and symbiotic algae to feed, but instead use large retractable polyps to catch and feed upon zooplankton. Place them in a shady spot and target-feed them with small shrimps by squirting frozen marine foods over them.

Elegance Coral, Catalaphyllia

Scientific name	Catalaphyllia spp.
Origin	Indo-Pacific.
Size	30cm.
Tank size	80cm.
Lighting	Moderate to bright.
Water flow	Moderate.
Ease of keeping	Moderate.
Special requirements	Space.

Notes – Elegance corals are beautiful large polyp stony corals that are in high demand. They can spread quite wide, and need to be placed low down in the aquarium or on the substrate so that they can spread properly, be seen in their full splendour, and don't fight with other corals that are placed too near to them. Usually an expensive purchase, make sure that water parameters are right before you add them.

APPENDICES

Conservation

As someone involved in the keeping of live animals, it's important that you respect them and their natural habitat. Understandably, many fishkeepers also become interested and involved in conservation.

Breed your own fish

Since many marine and tropical fish are still taken from the wild, it's important to research their requirements fully in order to provide a suitable home for them in captivity, and hopefully one in which they'll breed. Tank-bred fish relieve the pressure on populations in the wild and provide us with an insight into how they reproduce in their natural environment. Many fish are at greater risk from habitat destruction and the introduction of alien species than they are from being over-collected for the fishkeeping hobby. Indeed, some groups and species of fish, such as Goodieds for example, would be extinct if it weren't for the captive-breeding efforts of tropical fish hobbyists.

Having a healthy population of captive fish enables us not only to keep them for our leisure and enjoyment, but also ensures that if anything does happen to wild populations or their habitats the species won't be lost forever, and could even be reintroduced into the wild at some point in the future.

The same goes for new imports and fish that are available to hobbyists but have so far never been bred. These fish breed quite happily in the wild, so with the right conditions and stimuli they'll eventually breed in captivity too. Being the first in the world to captive-breed a species of fish is of importance to science, the hobby and the trade in that species, and could prove to be lucrative for you too.

Use less energy

Lowering our carbon footprint is important for all of us, and as fishkeepers we can certainly do our bit. By making a few small adjustments you can use less electricity. Check the wattage of your pumps and lighting, and look into buying and running more efficient versions – LED lighting, for instance, uses very little electricity, and by not containing any

number of ways to save on water-changes, though. The most obvious one is to have a smaller aquarium, such as a nano tank. Weekly water-changes will consist of a mere 10 litres, and changes of that volume won't even register on your water bill. Small water-changes are easier to carry out, more convenient, and won't break your back.

Look at your source of your water as well, and the type of water that your fish require. The most wasteful form of water is RO, as a huge percentage of it is waste water and normally runs away down the drain. Waste water can be used for other things, of course, such as for hardy freshwater fish, or even to water garden plants, but if you want to save water don't opt for a form of fishkeeping that requires RO.

Water-changes can be saved on in other ways too. Aquatic plants consume nitrate, the presence of which is the usual reason for us to change water in the first place. Failing that, nitrate-removal resins and denitrators (nitrate removing equipment) can be employed to keep water cleaner for longer.

Educate people

Just by showing a non-fishkeeper your fish tank you can teach them the importance of life underwater. It's through ignorance that many natural resources are lost, so by teaching someone that corals are live animals, for example, and not just bits of rock, those people may go on to educate other people and treat natural coral reefs as places to visit and treasure rather to plunder. If everyone knew as much about fish, corals and aquatic plants as fishkeepers do, more people would be proactive in actually preserving them for generations to come, and doing their bit to learn about them and protect them from extinction.

Enjoy your hobby!

Fishkeeping is a terrific hobby, and one that continues to grow across the world. And there's always more to learn. If you enjoy reading, there are books and magazines galore, not to mention dedicated Internet sites. Or you can join a local fish club or become active on an Internet forum and meet like-minded people.

Find a good aquatic shop and stick to it. Get to know the staff well and you'll get even better advice, and maybe even a discount. If you're really passionate you could even try working in the shop, where you'll be surrounded by hundreds of aquariums and thousands of fish on a daily basis.

Fishkeeping is accessible to everyone and it doesn't take long to become quite expert in a particular area. You might even decide to breed your fish and pass them on to other people to breed. Or you might display your fish at a show or enter your aquascape on an online 'tank of the month' competition.

When it comes to satisfaction there really is no better hobby than fishkeeping.

mercury its waste isn't hazardous either. Insulating the back and sides of your tropical aquarium means that less heat will be lost and the heater won't need to come on as often. And if you don't keep light-loving plants or corals, only turn the light on when you're sitting in front of the aquarium. Just a few hours of light per day is fine for all fish species, and will also help to prevent the proliferation of nuisance algae.

A very easy way to save electricity is to get a smaller aquarium in the first place. For instance, a 240-litre aquarium may have a 30W filter, a 200W heater and 80W of lighting, a total of 310W of usage. But a 30-litre aquarium may have a filter consuming 5W, a heater consuming 25W, and light consuming just 11W, the total usage coming in at just 41W, or a third less than a standard household light bulb. Smaller tanks also use less water, and filter media changes, dechlorinating and medicating are all less expensive. So by going small you save money as well as the planet.

Cheaper running costs benefit all of us, and there's nothing wrong with buying second-hand equipment, tanks and even fish. There's a healthy second-hand market in fishkeeping and lots of fish looking for a new home, so why not try it out? It could even be called recycling!

Buying locally-sourced fish saves energy too. The vast majority of aquarium fish are flown from tropical countries to the UK, USA and Europe, yet lots of them can actually be bred in the home aquarium and then traded. Tank-bred fish will definitely clock up far less air miles than farmed or wild-caught. Wherever possible buy from retailers who deal in locally-bred fish, not least because the fish are more likely to be from transport stress and disease.

Save water

Water-changes are vitally important for the well-being of your fish, and their welfare must come first. There are a

Glossary

Actinic light – Blue light used for illuminating marine aquariums, and simulating sunlight at depth in the sea. Corals benefit from Actinic light.

Aeration – The action of adding oxygen to water. Aeration is usually via an air pump, or a filter outlet, which agitates the surface of the water, adding oxygen.

Airstone – Connects to an airline, and at the other end, an air pump. An airstone diffuses air into water, oxygenating it.

Aquascaping – Landscaping, only under water. The art of arranging décor to make it look visually appealing.

Berlin system – A type of marine filtration system, using a protein skimmer and live rock. Possibly originated in Berlin, Germany.

Branching rock/Branch Rock – A type of live rock used for aquascaping marine aquariums. Made up of dead coral heads.

Calcareous – Containing lime, or calcium. Calcareous material was originally made in the seabed from dead shellfish and coral skeletons. Only suitable for marine and hard water/high pH freshwater tanks as it raises pH and GH.

Coldwater fish – fish that have evolved to naturally inhabit water with a temperature from 4–20C.

Cycling – The process of making an aquarium ready to hold fish, by adding bacteria to the filter.

Denitrator – A made up name for a piece of equipment that reduces nitrate levels, by harbouring denitrifying bacteria. Denitrifiers consume nitrates as food.

Detritivores – Tiny marine organisms that feed on organic waste. Useful in reef aquaria for keeping the tank tidy. Also eaten by fish.

DI- Deloniser. An Ion exchange resin inside a tube, that strips all minerals and pollutants from mains tap water, making it incredibly pure.

Drop checker – A small indicating device used in planted aquariums. Reactive liquid inside the drop checker changes colour with regard to how much carbon dioxide is in the water.

Dutch-style aquarium – A style of live plant decoration where plants are arranged in neat rows, like in a flowerbed.

Filtration – The removal of waste from water.

Floating base – A type of glass aquarium design where the bottom glass pane is held inside a protective outer frame.

FOWLR – Fish Only With Live Rock. A type of marine set-up where only fish and live rock are kept, with no corals or mobile invertebrates.

GH – General hardness. How much mineral content a water sample holds.

HID – A type of lighting used in aquariums. HID stands for High Intensity Discharge and is very bright. Metal halide lamps are HID.

HO – High Output, in reference to aquarium lighting, and brighter than standard output.

Ich – An abbreviation for *Ichthyophthirius multifiliis*, a freshwater fish parasite.

Inert materials – Decorative materials that do not leach any substances or alter the water chemistry.

Infusoria – Microscopic freshwater organisms which provide the first food for tiny fish fry.

Kelvin rating –The colour temperature, or colour spectrum of lighting is measured in units of Kelvin.

KH – From the German for Carbonate Hardness. A measurement of carbonates, or how much carbon dioxide is present in water.

Lph – Litres per hour. A common reference term used to measure the power of a water pump, or power filter.

LPS – Large Polyp Stony coral.

Marine fish – A fish that lives in the sea, and in salty sea water.

Media – Material used for filtering water. Sponge is a type of filter media.

Mulm – Liquefied muck and fish poo that builds up at the bottom of an aquarium or filter chamber.

Nano aquarium – A small aquarium, usually less than 100 litres total volume.

New tank syndrome – A phrase given to newly set-up tanks, experiencing water quality issues because too many fish have been added too soon, and insufficient bacteria are present to break down their waste.

Nitrate – A by-product of ammonia converting bacteria. Part of the natural, Nitrogen cycle.

Nitrite – Converted from ammonia by bacteria. Toxic to fish and present in aquariums where insufficient filter bacteria are present to convert harmful nitrite into less harmful nitrate.

Paludarium – A half-filled aquarium that is suitable for keeping amphibious plants and animals, which need areas of both water and land.

Reophilic fish – Freshwater fish that naturally inhabit rivers.

Reef bones – Branching/branch rock. Used in aquascaping marine aquariums, and originated in the sea as dead coral heads.

Refractometer – A high precision instrument for measuring how much salt is in sea water.

Refugium – A specially constructed area in a marine aquarium where tiny invertebrates and marine algae are encouraged, to aid the health of the system, only fish are not permitted as they would eat them.

Restrike – When light emitted from a light tube bounces off a reflector and back onto the tube, instead of into the aquarium below. A well designed light tube and reflector will have low restrike.

RO – Reverse Osmosis. A type of water purification where mains tap water is forced at pressure through a very fine membrane, removing minerals and pollutants as it goes. The pure water is then used in aquariums.

Skimmate – The dirty liquid that collects in the cup of a protein skimmer.

SPS – Small Polyp Stony coral.

Substrate – The fine, decorative sand or gravel placed on the bottom of aquariums.

Tropical fish – Freshwater and marine fish which naturally inhabit water with a temperature from 20–30°C.

Venturi – A bubble-making device which attaches to the outlet pipe of a power filter, and blows fine bubbles into aquarium water, aerating it as it goes.

VHO – Very High Output, in reference to aquarium lighting.

Index

NOTE: *Index is split into sections – General, Equipment, Fish and invertebrates and Plant species*